FROM GEORGE

... TO GEORGE

200 Years of Presidential Quotations

Republican Presidential Task Force

Photograph by David Valdez

Dear Member,

On behalf of the Presidential Task Force and our Republican Senators, I am pleased to present you with this special edition of *From George ... to George—200 Years of Presidential Quotations*, a collection of remarks and essays by me and the 40 other men who have served as Presidents from 1789 to 1989.

I am honored to be included in this historical treasury, and I am proud to have the oppportunity to share it with you. By working through the Task Force to elect Republican Senators, you've helped to extend our nation's 200-year legacy of freedom and economic opportunity into its third century.

From George ... to George—200 Years of Presidential Quotations documents the political wit and wisdom of our Presidents in a way that richly elaborates upon our nation's glorious history. Indeed, these quotations provide a unique and insightful record of our evolution as the freest society on earth. I hope this wonderful volume is as inspirational to you as it is to me.

Again, thank you for your continued support of the Republican Presidential Task force, and God bless you.

Sincerely,

[signature: George Bush]

FROM GEORGE

. . . TO GEORGE

200 Years of Presidential Quotations

Compiled by
Donald L. Miller and
John Sargent

with special assistance from
Jason L. Stern

ACKNOWLEDGEMENTS

Many individuals and institutions assisted us in the compilation of the quotations from our Presidents.

We are especially grateful to the Office of the President of the United States, the Office of Presidential Papers of the General Services Administration and the Library of Congress for their assistance.

A special thanks to several individuals from the Presidential Transition Office of the President-elect who helped us compile President Bush's quotations: Leslie Goodman and Emily Mead, who opened her treasury of information on President Bush. We would also like to thank C. Boyden Gray, Lee Atwater and Peter Roussel for their assistance.

The photograph is courtesy of David Valdez of the White House.

DEDICATED

TO

THE TRUE AMERICAN SOVEREIGN—

THE AMERICAN PEOPLE

INTRODUCTION

Each of us knows the all-time great quotations of our Presidents; but do you know who said them?

"No entangling alliances"[1]
"Malice toward none, with charity toward all"[2]
"The world must be made safe for democracy"[3]
"The only thing we have to fear is fear itself"[4]
"Ask not what your country can do for you; ask what you can do for your country"[5]

These quotes are but a few of the great statements made by our Presidents. Selected quotations from speeches, letters and press conferences offer unique insights into how America works, what makes our country run, the wisdom that guides national decisions and our role in the world of the future.

Quotations in this book have been taken from Presidents' papers and statements prior to, during and after their terms of office. Actual terms of office and biographical data for each President have been provided for your reference at the end of the book.

1. Thomas Jefferson. 2. Abraham Lincoln. 3. Woodrow Wilson.
4. Franklin D. Roosevelt. 5. John F. Kennedy.

TABLE OF CONTENTS

INTRODUCTION

HISTORIC PERSPECTIVE

THE GOVERNMENT

THE MARKETPLACE

THE PEOPLE

AREAS OF TRIAL

THE WORLD

THE FUTURE

THE PRESIDENTS

HISTORIC PERSPECTIVE

THE PRESIDENCY

A Presidency can shape an era—and it can change our lives. A successful Presidency can give meaning to an age.

> *George Bush*
> *1987*

I seek the Presidency to build a better America.

> *George Bush*
> *1988*

The foremost responsibility of any President is the national security of the United States and the encouragement of peace and freedom around the world.

> *George Bush*
> *1988*

I am a man who sees life in terms of missions— missions defined and missions completed.

> *George Bush*
> *1988*

The magnitude and difficulty of the trust ... overwhelms ... one.

> *George Washington*
> *1789*

It is a painful and thankless office.

> *Thomas Jefferson*
> *1796*

The second office of the government is honorable and easy, the first is but a splendid misery.

> *Thomas Jefferson*
> *1797*

It is preposterous to suppose that ... the President ... could better understand the wants and wishes of the people than their own representatives.
William Henry Harrison
1841

A person elected to that high office ... [the Presidency] ... must consider himself bound by the most solemn sanctions to guard, protect and defend the rights of all and of every portion, great or small, from the injustice and oppression of the rest.
William Henry Harrison
1841

Those who are called upon to administer it ... [the Presidency] ... must recognize as its leading principle the duty of shaping their measures so as to produce the greatest good for the greatest number.
William Henry Harrison
1841

No President who performs his duty faithfully and conscientiously can have any leisure.
James K. Polk
1848

The Presidency is ... a crown of thorns.
James Buchanan
1859

I must, in candor, say I do not think myself fit for the Presidency.
Abraham Lincoln
1859

Only events and not a man's exertions on his own behalf can make a President.
Abraham Lincoln
1859

While the people retain their virtue and vigilance, no Administration by any extreme of wickedness or folly can very seriously injure the Government in the short space of four years.
Abraham Lincoln
1861

It was my fortune or misfortune to be called to the Chief Magistracy without any prior political training.
Ulysses S. Grant
1876

I am not liked as President, by politicians in office, in the press, or in Congress.
Rutherford B. Hayes
1878

I look upon the next four years as a self- inflicted penance for the good of my country.
Grover Cleveland
1884

You don't live here [in the White House]. You are only Exhibit A to the country.
Theodore Roosevelt
1908

A President has a great chance; his position is that of a king and a prime minister rolled into one.
Theodore Roosevelt
1911

It isn't how long you are President that counts, but what you accomplish as President.
Theodore Roosevelt
1911

Anyone who has taken the oath I have just taken [oath of office of the President] must feel a heavy weight of responsibility. If not, he has no conception of the powers or duties of the office.
William H. Taft
1909

The Presidential office is ... an office in which a man must put on his war paint.
Woodrow Wilson
1908

The President is at liberty, both in law and conscience, to be as big a man as he can.
Woodrow Wilson
1908

I do not choose to run.
Calvin Coolidge
1927

The Presidency is ... the inspiring symbol of all that is highest in America's purposes and ideals.
Herbert Hoover
1928

My friends, the Presidency is not a prize to be won by mere glittering promises. It is not a commodity to be sold by high-pressure salesmanship and national advertising. The Presidency is a most sacred trust.
Franklin D. Roosevelt
1940

Being a President is like riding a tiger.
Harry S Truman
1945

Jefferson ... was a master politician, and this helped make him a great leader. A President has to be a politician in order to get the majority to go along with him on his program.

Harry S Truman
1945

To be President of the United States is to be lonely, very lonely at times.

Harry S Truman
1948

The President hears a hundred voices telling him that he is the greatest man in the world. He must listen very carefully indeed to hear the one voice that tells him he is not.

Harry S Truman
1948

The President is Chief of State. ... The bundle of burdens is unique; there is nothing else like it on the face of the earth.

Harry S Truman
1953

Ultimately, no President can master his responsibilities, save as his fellow citizens— indeed the whole people—comprehend the challenge of our times and move with him to meet it.

Harry S Truman
1953

The pressures and complexities of the Presidency have grown to a state where they are almost too much for one man to endure.

Harry S Truman
1956

A President, if he is to have a clear perspective and never get out of touch, must cut through the voices around him, know his history, and make certain of the reliability of the information he gets.
> *Harry S Truman*
> *1956*

The duties of the President are essentially endless.
> *Dwight D. Eisenhower*
> *1956*

The government of the United States has become too big, too complex, and too pervasive in its influence on all our lives for one individual to pretend to direct the details of its important and critical programming. Competent assistants are mandatory.
> *Dwight D. Eisenhower*
> *1960*

No man upon entering this office, regardless of his party, regardless of his previous service in Washington, could fail to be staggered upon learning ... the harsh enormity of the trials through which he must pass in the next four years. Each day the crises multiply. Each day their solution becomes more difficult.
> *John F. Kennedy*
> *1961*

We are not here to curse the darkness, but to light the candle that can guide us through that darkness to a safe and sane future.
> *John F. Kennedy*
> *1960*

No President can excuse or pardon the slightest deviation from irreproachable standards of behavior on the part of any member of the Executive Branch.
> *John F. Kennedy*
> *1961*

A President's hardest task is not to do what is right, but to know what is right. Yet, the Presidency brings no special gift of prophecy or foresight. You take an oath— step into an office— and you must then help to guide a great democracy.

Lyndon B. Johnson
1965

Every President lives, not only with what is, but with what has been, and what could be.

Lyndon B. Johnson
1969

Why would anyone want to be President today? The answer is not one of glory, or fame; today the burdens far outweigh its privileges. It's not because the Presidency offers a chance to be someone, but because it offers a chance to do something.

Richard M. Nixon
1968

Like President Washington ... I look forward to the status of private citizen with gladness and gratitude. To me, being a citizen of the United States of America is the greatest honor and privilege in the world.

Gerald R. Ford
1977

Most of the decisions that have to be made by a President are inherently not popular ones ... For the President to espouse a balanced program naturally arouses the condemnation, certainly the opposition ... of highly motivated opinion-shapers.

Jimmy Carter
1979

Only the most complex and difficult tasks come before me in the Oval Office. No easy answers are to be found there—because no easy questions come there.
Jimmy Carter
1980

The President of the United States is the steward of the nation's destiny.
Jimmy Carter
1980

THE AMERICAN REVOLUTION

I have no fear that the result of our experiment will be that men may be trusted to govern themselves without a master.
Thomas Jefferson
1787

Every man and every body of men on earth, possess the right of self-government.
Thomas Jefferson
1790

The Revolution was affected before the war commenced. The Revolution was in the minds and hearts of the people ... This radical change in the principles, opinions, sentiments and affections of the people was the real American Revolution.
John Adams
1818

The United States ... led the way in the overthrow of the feudal doctrine of perpetual allegiance.
Ulysses S. Grant
1873

(NOTE: Under feudal doctrine, a European government would claim that a citizen who emigrated to America and gave allegiance to the USA remained a citizen of the country of origin.)

America lives in the hearts of every man everywhere
who wishes to find a region where he will be free to work
out his destiny as he chooses.
Woodrow Wilson
1912

Today, 186 years later, that Declaration of Independence is still a revolutionary document. To read it today is
to hear a trumpet call. For that Declaration unleashed ... a
revolution in human affairs.
John F. Kennedy
1962

The revolution which began here in 1776 still runs
throughout the world ... All the forces which move and
shake our times have the power they do because of the
example of success offered by our American system.
Lyndon B. Johnson
1963

The American Revolution is also an unfinished enterprise. Each generation must do its part to carry on the
work.
Richard M. Nixon
1972

AMERICAN DOCTRINES

I believe in an America strong and prosperous, and
an America that lives by standards. An America of
honorable public service. An America that takes its
idealism and makes it concrete by acts of goodness. A
kinder, gentler nation. A tolerant America, enriched by
the contributions of many peoples and cultures.
George Bush
1988

This nation is a nation of principles.
George Bush
1986

We hold these truths to be self evident, that all men are created equal, that they are endowed by their Creator with certain inalienable rights, that among these are Life, Liberty and the Pursuit of Happiness.
Thomas Jefferson
The Declaration of Independence
1776

We, the People of the United States, in order to form a more perfect union ... do ordain and establish this Constitution for the United States of America.
The U.S. Constitution
1787

Congress shall make no law respecting an establishment of religion, or prohibiting the free exercise thereof ... No person shall be ... deprived of life, liberty or property without due process of law.
James Madison
from The Bill of Rights
1789

The American continents ... are henceforth not to be considered as subjects for future colonization by any European powers.
James Monroe
The Monroe Doctrine
1823

Open covenants of peace must be arrived at, after which ... diplomacy shall proceed always frankly and in the public view.
Woodrow Wilson
The Fourteen Points
1918

We look forward to a world founded upon four essential freedoms ... freedom of speech and expression ... freedom of every person to worship God in his own way ... freedom from want ... freedom from fear.

Franklin D. Roosevelt
The Four Freedoms
1941

The United States and Great Britain agree ... that their countries seek no aggrandizement ... no territorial changes that do not accord with the freely expressed wishes of the people concerned ... respect the right of all peoples to choose the form of government under which they will live ... believe that all nations must come to the abandonment of the use of force.

Franklin D. Roosevelt
British Prime Minister Winston Churchill
The Atlantic Charter
1941

In the field of world policy I would dedicate this nation to the policy of the good neighbor— the neighbor who resolutely respects himself and because he does so, respects the rights of others—the neighbor who respects his obligations and respects the sanctity of his agreements in and with a world of neighbors.

Franklin D. Roosevelt
The Good Neighbor Policy
1933

Totalitarian regimes imposed upon free peoples, by direct or indirect aggression, undermine the foundations of international peace and hence the security of the United States ... It must be the policy of the United States to support free peoples who are resisting attempted subjugation by armed minorities or by outside pressures ... I believe that our help should be primarily through economic and financial aid which is essential to economic

stability and orderly political processes.
> *Harry S Truman*
> *The Truman Doctrine*
> *1947*

Our concern for building a healthy world economy, ...
and ... for the maintenance of a civilization of free men
and institutions, all combine to give us ... great interest in
European recovery. ... These considerations led to the
suggestion by Secretary of State George Marshall on June
5, 1947 that further help be given only after the countries
of Europe had agreed upon their basic requirements and
the steps which they would take in order to give proper
effect to additional aid from us.
> *Harry S Truman*
> *The Marshall Plan*
> *1947*

Let every nation know, whether it wishes us well or ill,
that we shall pay any price, bear any burden, meet any
hardship, support any friend, oppose any foe, in order to
assure the survival and success of liberty.
> *John F. Kennedy*
> *1961*

Neither the defense nor the development of other
nations can be exclusively or primarily an American
undertaking. The nations of each part of the world should
assume the primary responsibility for their own well-
being and they themselves should determine the terms of
that well being.
> *Richard M. Nixon*
> *The Nixon Doctrine*
> *1970*

DEMOCRACY

When all is said and done, democracy depends on the soul of a people.
George Bush
1988

The promotion of freedom and democracy around the world is the bedrock principle of United States foreign policy.
George Bush
1987

Democracy has captured the spirit of our time. Like all forms of government, though it may be defended, democracy can never be imposed. We believe in democracy. For without doubt, though democracy may be a dream deferred for many, it remains, in my view, the destiny of man.
George Bush
1989

A government that remembers that the people are its master is a good and needed thing.
George Bush
1988

Democracy is the assertion of the right of the individual to live and to be treated justly as against any attempt on the part of any combination of individuals to make laws which will overburden him or which will destroy his equality among his fellows in the matter of right or privilege.
Woodrow Wilson
1920

The deeper purpose of democratic government is to assist ... its citizens ... to improve their conditions of life.
Franklin D. Roosevelt
1937

Democracy, the practice of self-government, is a covenant among free men to respect the rights and liberties of their fellows.
Franklin D. Roosevelt
1939

Democracy alone, of all forms of government, enlists the full force of men's enlightened will.
Franklin D. Roosevelt
1941

In a democratic world, as in a democratic nation, power must be linked to responsibility and be aligned to defend and justify itself within the framework of the general good.
Franklin D. Roosevelt
1945

Democracy is based on the conviction that man has moral and intellectual capacity, as well as the inalienable right, to govern himself with reason and justice.
Harry S Truman
1949

Democracy has proved that social justice can be achieved through peaceful change.
Harry S Truman
1949

Democracy, in one word ... is ... cooperation.
Dwight D. Eisenhower
1945

The dynamic of democracy is the power and purpose of the individual.
John F. Kennedy
1962

"I believe in democracy," said Woodrow Wilson, "because it releases the energy of every human being."
John F. Kennedy
1962

Freedom has many difficulties and democracy is not perfect, but we have never had to put up a wall to keep our people in, to prevent them from leaving us.
John F. Kennedy
"Ich bin ein Berliner" speech
1963

These echoes of history remind us of our roots and our strengths. They also remind us of that special genius of American democracy which at one critical point after another has led us to spot the new road to the future and given us the wisdom and courage to take it.
Richard M. Nixon
1970

FREEDOM

The United States must remain engaged around the world. If we are to support those who strive for freedom and democracy—and I believe we must—we cannot do it with words alone.
George Bush
1988

It is our spirit, the spirit of America—our faith in God, our willingness to stand for freedom, our commitment to defend freedom beyond our shores.
George Bush
1988

Freedom of religion, freedom of the press, freedom of the person under the protection of the habeas corpus; and trial by juries impartially selected—these principles form the bright constellation which has ... guided our steps through an age of revolution and transformation.
Thomas Jefferson
1801

Dissentions ... [are] ... perhaps inseparable from the enjoyment of freedom.
John Quincy Adams
1825

Our ideas of freedom came from many people. The greatest government of the world grew out of the inspiration, energy and ideas which were brought here by the English, the Scotch, the Irish, the Danes, the Swedes, the Germans, the Poles, the Jews, the Italians and others who came to these shores in search of freedom.
Harry S Truman
1956

The most powerful single force in the world today is neither communism nor capitalism, neither the H-bomb nor the guided missile—it is man's eternal desire to be free and independent.
John F. Kennedy
1957

The unity of freedom has never relied upon uniformity of opinion.
John F. Kennedy
1963

The essence of freedom is that each of us shares in the shaping of his own destiny.
Richard M. Nixon
1969

Freedom is not the sole prerogative of a lucky few, but the inalienable and universal right of all human beings.
> *Ronald Reagan*
> *1982*

LIBERTY

We are a nation that was founded for liberty and human rights—for the freedom to speak and assemble and worship, each in our own way. This is our heritage—one that we must never abandon for the expediency of the moment.
> *George Bush*
> *1987*

The sacred fire of liberty and the destiny of the republican model of government are ... deeply and finally staked on the experiment entrusted to the hands of the American people.
> *George Washington*
> *1789*

The way to secure liberty is to give them ... [the people] ... power at all times to defend it in the legislature and in the courts of justice.
> *John Adams*
> *1787*

The last hope of human liberty in this world rests on us.
> *Thomas Jefferson*
> *1811*

The God who gave us life, gave us liberty.
> *Thomas Jefferson*
> *1808*

I would define liberty to be a power to do as we would be done by. The definition of liberty to be the power of doing whatever the law permits ... does not seem satisfactory.

John Quincy Adams
1825

Without union our independence and liberty would never have been achieved.

Andrew Jackson
1833

In entering into society, individuals must give up a share of liberty to preserve the rest.

Andrew Jackson
1833

Eternal vigilance by the people is the price of liberty.

Andrew Jackson
1837

Liberty unregulated by law degenerates into anarchy.

Millard Fillmore
1852

The history of liberty is a history of limitations of governmental power, not the increase of it.

Woodrow Wilson
1912

The man who seeks freedom from ... responsibility in the name of individual liberty is either fooling himself or trying to cheat his fellow man. He wants to eat the fruits of orderly society without paying for them.

Franklin D. Roosevelt
1938

As Lincoln said, the Declaration of Independence, "gave liberty not alone to the people of this country, but hope to all the world."
John F. Kennedy
1959

The world is now waiting for us to reapply the faith we inherited from our fathers, and to give them a new creative validity in the uncharted world that surrounds us.
John F. Kennedy
1960

We were never meant to be an oasis of liberty and abundance in a worldwide desert of disappointed dreams.
Lyndon B. Johnson
1965

POLITICAL MAXIMS

A campaign is a disagreement, and disagreements divide. But an election is a decision, and decisions clear the way for harmony and peace.
George Bush
1988

Public service is the highest calling ... those who take on the people's trust must hold themselves to an exacting code of conduct ...
George Bush
1988

The due administration of justice is the firmest pillar of good government.
George Washington
1789

I have sworn upon the altar of God eternal hostility against every form of tyranny over the mind of man.
Thomas Jefferson
1787

Political dissention is ... a less evil than the lethargy of despotisms.
Thomas Jefferson
1797

The will of the people is the only legitimate foundation of any government.
Thomas Jefferson
1801

Error of opinion may be tolerated where reason is left free to combat it.
Thomas Jefferson
1801

There is no grievance that is a fit object of redress by mob rule.
Abraham Lincoln
1837

No system of legislation can be wise which is fluctuating and uncertain.
John Tyler
1842

The true rule in determining to embrace anything is not whether it has any evil in it; but whether it has more evil than good. There are few things wholly evil or wholly good. Almost everything, especially of governmental policy, is an inseparable compound of the two.
Abraham Lincoln
1848

Stand with anybody that stands right. Stand with him when he is right and part with him when he goes wrong.
   Abraham Lincoln
   1854

The love of property and consciousness of right or wrong have conflicting places in our organization, which often make a man's life seem ... a riddle.
   Abraham Lincoln
   1860

Public virtue is the vital spirit of republics, and history proves that when this has decayed and the love of money has usurped its place, although the forms of free government may remain for a season, the substance has departed forever.
   James Buchanan
   1857

What is the use of being elected or re-elected unless you stand for something?
   Grover Cleveland
   1887

Our mission is not punishment, but the rectification of wrong.
   Grover Cleveland
   1893

What is it that America stands for? ... It is the sovereignty of self-governing people.
   Woodrow Wilson
   1916

It is not the name of the action, but the result of the action, which is of chief concern.
   Calvin Coolidge
   1925

The only thing we have to fear is fear itself—nameless, unreasoning, unjustified terror which paralyzes needed efforts to convert retreat into advance.
Franklin D. Roosevelt
1933

The life of a nation is the fullness and the measure of its will to live.
Franklin D. Roosevelt
1941

A government can strive ... to maintain an economic system whose doors are open to enterprise and ambition, ... but enterprise and ambition are qualities which no government can supply ... A government can sincerely strive for peace, ... but no government can place peace in the hearts of foreign rulers ... No government can inoculate its people against the fatal materialism that plagues our age.
Dwight D. Eisenhower
1954

A Government that is strong, a government that is compassionate is the kind of Government that endures.
Lyndon B. Johnson
1964

Self-righteous indignation is not a policy.
Lyndon B. Johnson
1964

No better words could describe our present course ... than those once spoken by Thomas Jefferson: "It is the melancholy law of human societies to be compelled sometimes to choose a great evil in order to ward off a greater; to deter their neighbors from rapine by making it cost more than honest gain."
Lyndon B. Johnson
1967

Skeptics do not build societies; the idealists are the builders.
Richard Nixon
1969

Morality in its broadest sense, ... [is] ... a set of standards by which the community chooses to judge itself.
Richard Nixon
1969

Each generation ... has to face circumstances not of its own choosing, but by which its character is measured and its spirit tested.
Jimmy Carter
1976

The best organized government will only be as effective as the people who carry out the policy.
Jimmy Carter
1978

Honorable men and women can honestly disagree. They can also leave their disagreements behind them. Let's have our differences behind us and get on with the nation's business.
Ronald Reagan
1982

THE GOVERNMENT

THE AMERICAN SYSTEM

Government functions best as a catalyst, not a cure. We need a smarter, more efficient government, not a bigger one.
George Bush
1988

It is of great importance ... not only to guard the society against the oppression of its rulers, but to guard one part of the society against the injustice of the other part ... If a majority is united by a common interest, the rights of the minority will be insecure ... In the federal republic of the United States ... the society itself will be broken into so many parts, interests and classes of citizens, that the rights of the minority will be in little danger from interested combinations of the majority.
James Madison
1787

In this great nation there is but one order, that of the people ... The whole system is elective, the complete sovereignty being in the people, and every officer in every department deriving his authority from and being responsible to them for his conduct.
James Monroe
1821

The General Government of the Union and the separate governments of the States are all sovereignties of limited powers, fellow servants of the same masters.
John Quincy Adams
1825

As long as our Government is administered for the good of the people, and is well regulated by their will; as long as it secures to us the rights of person and property, liberty of conscience and of the press, it will be worth defending.
Andrew Jackson
1829

The thoughtful framers of our Constitution legislated for our country as they found it ... Distinct sovereignties were already in actual existence, whose cordial union was essential to the welfare and happiness of all. Between many of them there was, at least to some extent, a real diversity of interests, ... they differed in size, in population, in wealth, and in actual and potential resources and power; they varied in the character of their industry and staple productions, and ... [in some] ... existed domestic institutions which, unwisely disturbed, might endanger the harmony of the whole.
Martin van Buren
1837

The Government of the United States is one of delegated and limited powers.
James K. Polk
1845

A majority held in restraint by constitutional checks and limitations, and always changing easily with deliberate changes of popular opinions and sentiments, is the only true sovereign of a free people. Whoever rejects it does, of necessity, fly to anarchy or despotism.
Abraham Lincoln
1861

By the Father of his Country, our Constitution was recommended for adoption as "the result of a spirit of amity and mutual concession." In the same spirit it should be administered.
  Grover Cleveland
  1885

We have ... a system of individualism peculiarly our own which must not be forgotten in any governmental acts, for from it have grown greater accomplishments than those of any other nation.
  Herbert Hoover
  1932

At the heart of our American system is ... the ideal that there shall be an opportunity in life, and equal opportunity, for every boy and girl, every man and woman. It holds that they have the chance to rise to any position to which their character and ability may entitle them.
  Herbert Hoover
  1936

Our Constitution wisely assigns both joint and separate roles to each branch of the Government; and a President and a Congress who hold each other in mutual respect will neither permit nor attempt any trespass.
  John F. Kennedy
  1961

What has made America great has not been what government has done for the people, but what the people have done for themselves.
  Richard Nixon
  1968

We have a Constitution which sets limits on what government can do, but that allows wide discretion within those limits. We have a system of divided powers, of checks and balances, of periodic elections, all of which are designed to ensure that the majority has a chance to work its will—but not to override the rights of the minority, or to infringe the rights of the individual. What this adds up to is a democratic process.
Richard Nixon
1969

FEDERALISM

To achieve quality results, we must set and enforce standards, provide incentives, and permit the freedom and flexibility on the local level to experiment with new ideas.
George Bush
1988

There are four things, which are essential ... [one is] ... An indissoluble union of States under one federal head.
George Washington
1783

Our country is too large to have all its affairs directed by a single government.
Thomas Jefferson
1800

I deem ... the support of the State governments in all their rights, as the most competent administrations for our domestic concerns.
Thomas Jefferson
1801

(NOTE: Federalism is the allocation of powers and responsibilities among different levels of government.)

The powers delegated ... to the Federal Government are few and defined. Those which are to remain in the State governments are numerous and indefinite. The former will be exercised primarily on external objects, as war, peace, negotiation and foreign commerce ... The powers reserved to the several States will extend to all the objects which ... concern the lives, liberties and properties of the people.

James Madison
1788

In proportion as the Federal Government encroaches upon the rights of the States, in the same proportion does it impair its own power and detract from its ability to fulfill the purposes of its creation.

Andrew Jackson
1833

Our constitutional liberty rests upon a proper distribution of power between the State and Federal authorities.

Franklin Pierce
1853

If the Federal Government will confine itself to the exercise of powers clearly granted by the Constitution, it can hardly happen that its action upon any question should endanger the institutions of the States or interfere with their right to manage matters strictly domestic according to the will of their own people.

Franklin Pierce
1853

There is an ... important field of cooperation by the Federal Government with the multitude of agencies, State, municipal and private, in the systematic development of those processes which effect health, recreation, education and the home.

Herbert Hoover
1929

We cannot conduct a national government after the practice of 1787, 1837 or 1887, for the obvious reason that human needs and human desires are infinitely greater, infinitely more difficult to meet than in any previous period in the life of our Republic.
  Franklin D. Roosevelt
  1938

Communities ... [are] ... where the everlasting job of building a stronger America must have its roots ... To do so, we rely on the good sense and local knowledge of the community and will, therefore, decentralize administration as much as possible so that the services of government may be closer to you and thus serve you better.
  Dwight D. Eisenhower
  1954

Balance of power is essential to our form of free society. If you take the centralization short-cut, ... you will perhaps get quick action. But there is no perhaps about the price you will pay; ... the growth of a swollen, bureaucratic, monster Government in Washington in whose shadow our State and local governments will ultimately wither and die.
  Dwight D. Eisenhower
  1956

After a third of a century concentrating power, an old idea is winning acceptance: the idea that what we need is a dispersal of power.
  Richard Nixon
  1968

In my State of the Union Address nearly two years ago, I outlined a program which I described as a "New American Revolution"—a peaceful revolution in which

power ... [is] ... returned back to the people ... a revolution as far-reaching, as exciting as that first revolution
almost 200 years ago.
  Richard Nixon
  1972

   After 40 years of unprecedented expansion of the
Federal Government, the time has come to redress the
balance—to shift more responsibility and power back to
the states and localities and, most important, to the people
all across America.
  Richard Nixon
  1972

   We must strike a new balance in our system of Federalism—a balance that favors greater responsibility and
freedom for the leaders of our State and local governments.
  Gerald R. Ford
  1972

   Centralization of power in the hands of the Federal
Government did not happen by accident. Over the years
local officials helped create this power flow by turning to
the Federal Government for solutions to local problems ...
Now you are becoming more aware that to get a job done,
the very last thing you should ask for is Federal money ...
What we must do is strive to recapture the bounty of vigor
and optimism de Tocqueville found in American cities.
We can start by re-establishing the proper relationship
between the Federal, State and local governments.
  Ronald Reagan
  1981

Our next major undertaking must be a program to ... make our system of federalism work again ... Our citizens feel they've lost control of even the most basic decisions made about the essential services of government, such as schools, welfare, roads and even garbage ... Well, let's solve this problem with a bold stroke: the return of some 47 billion dollars in federal programs to state and local governments, together with the means to finance them.
    Ronald Reagan
    1982

POLITICS/POLITICIANS

You know, politics is nothing more—or less—than philosophy translated into action.
    George Bush
    1987

Politics is all about risk and reward. One risk you always face in politics is that you're going to lose ... but the reward is great if you succeed—the opportunity to make a difference and give something back to this country that has given us all so much, to have a disproportionate chance to shape events, to fight for the principles you believe in.
    George Bush
    1988

Men in political life must be ambitious.
    Rutherford B. Hayes
    1888

The great preacher reaches the heart of his hearers not by knowledge but by ... showing himself a brother man to his fellow man.
    Woodrow Wilson
    1897

The science of politics ... may properly be said to be ... the adjustment of conflicting group interest.
>   *Franklin D. Roosevelt*
>   *1936*

Any good politician with nerve and a program that is right can win in the face of the stiffest opposition.
>   *Harry S Truman*
>   *1948*

A professional politician's first duty is to appeal to the forces that unite us, and to channel the forces that divide us into paths where a democratic solution is possible.
>   Lyndon B. Johnson
>   *1963*

POWER

I believe that power must always be kept close to the individual—close to the hands that raise the family and run the home.
>   ***George Bush***
>   ***1988***

The jaws of power are always open to devour.
>   *John Adams*
>   *1765*

Nip the shoots of arbitrary power in the bud is the only maxim which can ever preserve the liberties of any people.
>   *John Adams*
>   *1775*

The accumulation of all powers, legislative, executive and judiciary, in the same hands ... may justly be pronounced the very definition of tyranny.
>   *James Madison*
>   *1792*

The tenure of power by man is, in the moral purposes of his Creator, upon condition that it shall be exercised to ends of beneficence, to improve the condition of himself and his fellow man.
John Quincy Adams
1825

Irresponsible power of itself excites distrust.
Martin van Buren
1826

The more power is divided, the more irresponsible it becomes.
Woodrow Wilson
1885

The danger of American democracy lies not in ... the concentration of administrative power in responsible ... hands. It lies in having the power insufficiently concentrated so that no one can be held responsible.
Theodore Roosevelt
1908

They talk of my power! My power vanishes into thin air the instant that my fellow citizens ... cease to believe that I represent them.
Theodore Roosevelt
1910

Power consists in one's capacity to link his will with the purposes of others, to lead by reason and a gift of cooperation.
Woodrow Wilson
1913

As intricacies of human relationships increase, so power to govern them must also increase.
Franklin D. Roosevelt
1937

THE MARKETPLACE

PRIVATE ENTERPRISE

Risk-taking is the heartbeat of the American dream. Whether as a business or an individual, you have to take risks to grow. And when people take chances—expanding an existing business or creating a new one—the whole economy grows. The rewards flow not just to investors, but the society as a whole—in the form of jobs and economic growth.
George Bush
1988

Small business is the engine of the American economy—one of the greatest job-creating business machines anywhere.
George Bush
1988

We are experiencing the greatest change in the American economy since the industrial revolution ... The great American job creating machine has churned out 17 million new jobs since 1982 ...
I believe that change is inevitable and exciting. Government must not mandate how society responds. Let's give people the tools to make better choices in a changing society. Let's give people the opportunity for a better life ... That's what drew people to America centuries ago ... that's what stirs us all.
George Bush
1988

Commerce has made this country what it is, and it cannot be destroyed or neglected without involving the people in poverty and distress.
John Adams
1797

Agriculture, manufacture, commerce and navigation, the four pillars of our prosperity, are the most thriving when left most free to individual enterprise.
Thomas Jefferson
1801

Our manufacturers will likewise require the systematic and fostering care of the Government ... The capital which nourishes our manufacturers should be domestic ... Equally important is it to provide at home a market for our raw materials.
James Monroe
1817

The merchant, the shipmaster, and the manufacturer discovered and disclosed to our statesmen that commercial emancipation must be added to the political freedom which had been so bravely won.
Benjamin Harrison
1889

The prudent capitalist will never venture his capital in manufacturing ... or in any other ... pursuit ... , if there exists a state of uncertainty as to whether the Government will repeal tomorrow what it has enacted today.
John Tyler
1842

Our manufacturers are rapidly making us industrially independent, and are opening to capital and labor new and profitable fields of employment.
James A. Garfield
1881

No country can long endure if its foundations are not laid deep in the material prosperity which grows, from thrift, from business energy and enterprise.
Theodore Roosevelt
1899

The originative part of America, the part of America that makes new enterprises, the part into which the ambitious and gifted workingman makes his way up, the class that saves, that plans, that organizes, that presently spreads its enterprises until they have national scope and character—that middle class is being more and more squeezed out by the processes which we have been taught to call prosperity.
Woodrow Wilson
1912

The chief business of America is business.
Calvin Coolidge
1925

American business needs a lifting purpose greater than the struggle for materialism.
Herbert Hoover
1925

The background of our American system and the motivation of progress is essentially that we should allow free play of social and economic forces as far as will not limit equality of opportunity.
Herbert Hoover
1932

I will always believe in private enterprise as the backbone of well-being in the United States.
Franklin D. Roosevelt
1936

Government has a final responsibility for the well-being of its citizenship. If private cooperative endeavor fails to provide work for willing hands and relief for the unfortunate, those suffering hardship from no fault of their own have a right to call upon Government for aid; and a government worthy of the name must make a fitting response.
Franklin D. Roosevelt
1938

Our policy is, of course, to rely as much as possible on private enterprise to provide jobs.
Franklin D. Roosevelt
1945

Businessmen must continue to have incentives ... for investment and for the development of new lines of enterprise.
Harry S Truman
1950

The prosperity of our small business enterprises is an indispensable element in the maintenance of our economic strength. Creation of the Small Business Administration and tax laws facilitating small business expansion are but two of the many steps this Government has taken to encourage smaller enterprises.
Dwight D. Eisenhower
1955

Our competitive enterprise system depends upon the energy of free human beings, limited by prudent restraints in law, using free markets to plan, organize and distribute production, and spurred by the prospect of reward for successful effort.
Dwight D. Eisenhower
1956

It is ... difficult to know ... how the Nation can survive unless the Government and business and all other groups in the country are exerting their best effort in an atmosphere of understanding and, I hope, cooperation.
John F. Kennedy
1962

If we are to have the full blessings of free enterprise, business and labor must place the fundamental national interest first.
Lyndon B. Johnson
1967

Government should try to make the enterprise system work better, not try to supplant it with central direction. The rule should be: as much freedom as possible, as little intervention as needed.
Richard Nixon
1960

Seeking the freedom to control their own lives and economic destinies, hundreds of merchants and shopkeepers and craftsmen helped wage and win the fight for America's independence. With that independence, small business has played a major role in building America to greatness in the two centuries that have followed.
Gerald R. Ford
1976

Five out of six jobs in this country are in private business and industry. Common sense tells us this is the place to look for more jobs and to find them faster.
Gerald R. Ford
1976

Through their insistence on the free enterprise system, our forefathers unleashed the creative energies of a people, built the foundation for our unparalleled political and economic freedom, and brought forth a vital force in the world.
> *Ronald Reagan*
> *1981*

We who live in free market societies believe that growth, prosperity and, ultimately, human fulfillment are created from the bottom up, not the government down. Only when the human spirit is allowed to invent and create, only when individuals are given a stake in deciding economic policies and benefiting from their success—only then can societies remain economically alive, dynamic, prosperous, progressive and free.
> *Ronald Reagan*
> *1981*

LABOR

Some say American workers can't compete any more, but I don't buy that for a minute. American workers are the best in the world. If we give them the tools, they can compete, and they will prevail.
> *George Bush*
> *1988*

I believe the best policy is to unleash the most powerful force on earth: the power of individual workers, individual entrepreneurs, and individual dreamers. Why do I believe this? Because it works.
> *George Bush*
> *1988*

Our ancestors who migrated here were laborers, not lawyers.
> *Thomas Jefferson*
> *1774*

Free labor has the inspiration of hope.
   Abraham Lincoln
   1859

The habits of our whole species fall into three great
classes—useful labor, useless labor and idleness. Of these,
the first only is meritorious; and to it all the products of
labor rightfully belong.
   Abraham Lincoln
   1847

There is no permanent class of hired laborers among
us. Twenty-five years ago I was a hired laborer. The
hired laborer of yesterday labors on his own account
today; and will hire others to labor for him tomorrow.
Advancement—improvement in condition—is the order of
things in a society of equals.
   Abraham Lincoln
   1859

Work is honorable; it is entitled to an honorable rec-
ompense.
   Calvin Coolidge
   1926

In the case of labor as in the case of capital ... we seek
cooperation. In every case power and responsibility must
go hand in hand.
   Franklin D. Roosevelt
   1938

I believe now, as I have all my life, in the right of
workers to join unions and to protect their unions.
   Franklin D. Roosevelt
   1943

Working people in America value family, work and neighborhood. These are the things we have in common ... When it comes to the bottom line, all of us are striving for the same thing—a strong and healthy America and a fair shake for the working people.
Ronald Reagan
1981

I am the first man to attain this high office who was formerly president of an AFL-CIO union ... I participated as a negotiator, ... and as president led the Guild in its first major strike. Our policy has been and will continue to be: What is good for the American worker is good for America.
Ronald Reagan
1981

PROSPERITY

The fact is prosperity is not an end, but a beginning. It has a point: It gives us time to think and care; it frees us up to learn, to grow, to be better than we are, to develop the things of the spirit and the heart.
George Bush
1987

We have to remember that prosperity has a purpose, and it's to pursue the better angels of our nature. To make greater strides in improving education and cleaning up the environment, in building the arts and sciences and the things of the spirit—to give a helping hand to a fellow citizen who needs it.
George Bush
1988

It is a kind of law of nature that every nation prospers by the prosperity of others.
Thomas Jefferson
1816

At the basis of all prosperity ... lies the improvement
of the intellectual and moral condition of the people.
> *Rutherford B. Hayes*
> *1877*

I understand prosperity to be the abundant, intelligent,
economic development of resources possessed by the
country itself.
> *Woodrow Wilson*
> *1912*

The end of government is to keep open the opportunity for a more abundant life.
> *Calvin Coolidge*
> *1928*

This country is in the midst of an era of prosperity ...
But, having reached this position, we should not fail to
comprehend that it can easily be lost.
> *Calvin Coolidge*
> *1928*

Prosperity cannot be restored by raids upon the public
treasury.
> *Herbert Hoover*
> *1930*

Investment for prosperity can be made in a democracy.
> *Franklin D. Roosevelt*
> *1939*

The view of this government is that, in the long run,
our economic prosperity and the prosperity of the whole
world are best served by the elimination of artificial
barriers to international trade.
> *Harry S Truman*
> *1946*

We are in the midst of the greatest upsurge of economic well being in the history of any nation ... We
worked for two centuries to climb this peak of prosperity,
but we are only at the beginning of the road to the Great
Society.
Lyndon B. Johnson
1965

Prosperity without war requires action on three fronts.
We must have more and better jobs; we must stop the rise
in the cost of living; we must protect the dollar from the
attacks of international money speculators.
Richard Nixon
1971

If living standards are to rise, productivity must
grow—there's no way around this as an economic fact of
life.
Jimmy Carter
1980

Take advantage of the genius of our economic system—a system as Walter Lippmann observed 40 years
ago, which for the first time in history gave men "a way of
producing wealth in which the good fortune of others
multiplied their own."
Ronald Reagan
1981

The societies which have achieved the most broad-
based economic progress in the shortest period of time are
not the most tightly controlled, not necessarily the biggest
in size, or the wealthiest in natural resources. No, what
unites them all is their willingness to believe in the magic
of the marketplace.
Ronald Reagan
1981

THE PEOPLE

THE PEOPLE AS THEY ARE

I think Americans are in fairly general agreement as to what constitutes good character and ethical behavior. It includes such qualities as decency, fairness, honesty, duty, tolerance, courage, self-discipline and respect for the law.
George Bush
1987

We must bear up and make the best of mankind as they are, since we cannot have them as we wish.
George Washington
1775

Men ... are ... divided into two parties. Those who fear and distrust the people. ... Those who identify ... with the people, ... and consider them as the most honest and safe ... depository of the public interest.
Thomas Jefferson
1824

In all that the people can individually do for themselves, the government ought not interfere.
Abraham Lincoln
1854

No man is good enough to govern another man without that other's consent.
Abraham Lincoln
1854

I do not deny the possibility that the people may err in an election, but, if they do, the true ... [remedy] ... is in the next election.
Abraham Lincoln
1861

The voters of the Union, who make and unmake constitutions, and upon whom will hang the destinies of our governments, can transmit their supreme authority to no successors save the coming generation of voters, who are the sole heirs of sovereign power.
James A. Garfield
1881

Every voter, as surely as your Chief Magistrate, ... exercises a public trust.
Grover Cleveland
1885

The success of our popular government rests wholly upon the correct interpretation of the deliberate, intelligent, dependable popular will of America.
Warren G. Harding
1921

We do not believe that men exist merely to strengthen the state or be cogs in an economic machine. We do believe that governments are created to serve the people.
Harry S Truman
1948

A people that values its privileges above its principles soon loses both.
Dwight D. Eisenhower
1953

The aspirations of most of our people can best be fulfilled through their own enterprise and initiative, without Government interference.
Dwight D. Eisenhower
1955

America did not become great through softness and self-indulgence.
Dwight D. Eisenhower
1960

The American, by nature, is optimistic ... experimental, an inventor and a builder ... Arouse his will to believe in himself, give him a great goal to believe in, and he will create the means to reach it.
   John F. Kennedy
   1960

Our primary aim must be not to help government but to help the people—to help people attain the life they deserve.
   Richard Nixon
   1960

Americans are always at their best when the challenge is greatest.
   Richard Nixon
   1960

The American dream does not come to those who fall asleep.
   Richard Nixon
   1969

The greatest privilege a person can have is to serve in a cause bigger than himself.
   Richard Nixon
   1970

We build our economy, after all, not to create cold, impersonal statistics for the record books, but to better the lives of our people.
   Richard Nixon
   1973

The best organized government will only be as effective as the people who carry out its policy.
   Jimmy Carter
   1978

Man's unsatisfied aspiration for economic progress and social justice can best be achieved by free men working within a framework of democratic institutions.
Ronald Reagan
1982

EDUCATION

Educational achievement has less to do with money or class-size than ... with homework assigned and completed ... Hard work, a respect for learning and self-discipline—these qualities are not just how you learn in school, they're also what you learn ... They are the values that lead to success.
George Bush
1987

As Martin Luther King once said, "We must remember that intelligence is not enough. Intelligence plus character—that is the goal of true education.
Good education is good policy, and it is good politics. In the years ahead, education can be our most powerful economic program—our most important trade program—our most effective urban program—our best program for producing jobs and bringing people out of poverty. The best investment we can make is in our children.
George Bush
1987

The challenge of the future will not be finding jobs for our people—it will be finding people for our jobs. Our world is evolving rapidly into a high-tech, information-based work place that demands a good education ... Young people who turn their backs on school not only lose their place at the starting line, they take themselves out of the game and our whole society suffers.
George Bush
1988

Knowledge is in every country the surest basis of public happiness.
George Washington
1790

To the security of a free constitution ... [education] ... contributes ... by teaching the people themselves to know and to value their own rights.
George Washington
1790

I have proposed ... establishing a national university. A primary object ... should be the education of our youth in the sciences of government.
George Washington
1796

Education is here placed among the articles of public care, not that it would be proposed to take its ordinary branches out of the hands of private enterprise, ... but a public institution can alone supply those sciences which ... though rarely called for are yet necessary ... to the improvement of the country and some of them to its preservation.
Thomas Jefferson
1806

This institution [the University of Virginia] will be based on the illimitable freedom of the human mind. For here we are not afraid to follow truth wherever it may lead, nor tolerate error so long as reason is left free to combat it.
Thomas Jefferson
1820

I look to the diffusion of ... education as the resource most to be relied upon for ameliorating the condition, promoting the virtue, and advancing the happiness of man.
Thomas Jefferson
1822

I desire to see the time when education and by its means, morality, sobriety, enterprise and industry, shall become much more general than at present.
Abraham Lincoln
1832

Next important to freedom and justice is popular education, without which neither freedom nor justice can be permanently maintained.
James A. Garfield
1880

The interest of the General Government in the education of the people found an early expression, not only in ... utterances of our ablest statesmen, but in liberal appropriations from the common resources ... No one will deny that ... those who hold the ultimate control of all public affairs should have the necessary intelligence to wisely direct and determine them.
Benjamin Harrison
1889

A grave peril to the Republic would be a citizenship too ignorant to understand ... the great value ... of our institutions and laws ... Nor must we be unmindful of the need ... [to] ... encourage the spread of knowledge and free education.
William McKinley
1897

The object of a liberal training is not learning, but discipline and the enlightenment of the mind.
Woodrow Wilson
1909

Education is for the purpose of bringing to bear the experiences of the past in finding solutions of the problems of the present.
Calvin Coolidge
1920

We cannot hope to succeed in directing this increasingly complex civilization unless we can draw the talent of leadership from the whole people ... The full opportunity of every boy and girl to rise through the selective processes of education can alone secure to us this leadership.
Herbert Hoover
1929

This country is great enough to guarantee the right to education adequate for full citizenship.
Franklin D. Roosevelt
1945

Health and education have their beginning in the home.
Harry S Truman
1948

The fundamental purpose of our educational system is to instill a moral code in the rising generation and create a citizenship which will be responsible for the welfare of the Nation.
Harry S Truman
1949

There is no limit to knowledge. A person learns as long as he lives.
Harry S Truman
1956

We must have teachers of competence. To obtain and hold them we need standards. We need a national goal.
Dwight D. Eisenhower
1959

A child miseducated is a child lost. The damage cannot be repaired. Civilization, ran an old saying, is a race between education and catastrophe.
John F. Kennedy
1962

When the youngest child alive today has grown to the cares of manhood, our position in the world will be determined first of all by what provisions we make today—for his education, his health, and his opportunities for a good home and a good job and a good life.
John F. Kennedy
1962

Education is the mainspring of our economic and social progress.
John F. Kennedy
1962

Education is the key that unlocks progress in the struggle against hunger and want and injustice ... Above all else, it is the wellspring of freedom and peace.
Lyndon B. Johnson
1961

Jobs which once could be filled by strength and native intelligence now call for a college degree. We have truly entered the Century of the Educated Man.
Lyndon B. Johnson
1963

Jefferson knew the destiny of America was inseparable from education ... Now ... we know a sterner truth ...

Education, long the key to opportunity and fulfillment, is today also the key to survival.
Richard Nixon
1968

There is no easy way to excellence, no short cut to the truth, no magic wand that can produce a trained and disciplined mind without the hard discipline of learning.
Richard Nixon
1969

A nation's values are only as lasting as the ability of each generation to pass them on to the next.
Richard Nixon
1969

Education is the insurance we have to provide the talent and capability to meet every demand on our National agenda. The challenge of the 80's in education is to see that quantity education becomes quality education.
Jimmy Carter
1980

The American people have always recognized that education is one of the soundest investments they can make.
Jimmy Carter
1981

As a Nation, we are dedicated to excellence in education. It makes a better life for our children as individuals, and it further secures the liberty which we cherish. As James Madison said: "Knowledge will forever govern ignorance. And a people who mean to be their own Governors, must arm themselves with the power which knowledge gives."
Ronald Reagan
1981

HAPPINESS

There is no Truth more thoroughly established than that there exists ... an indissoluble union between virtue and happiness.
George Washington
1789

We hold these Truths to be self-evident, that all Men are created equal, that they are endowed by their Creator with certain inalienable rights, that among these are Life, Liberty and the Pursuit of Happiness.
Thomas Jefferson
1776

The freedom and happiness of man ... are the sole objects of all legitimate government.
Thomas Jefferson
1810

Without virtue, happiness cannot be.
Thomas Jefferson
1816

The happiness of the people, the great end of man, is the end of government.
John Adams
1776

Sound morals, religious liberty and a just sense of ... responsibility are essentially connected with all true ... happiness.
William Henry Harrison
1841

Property should not be the object of government, but the life, liberty and happiness of the people.
Andrew Johnson
1845

Happiness lies not in the mere possession of money; it lies in the joy of achievement, in the thrill of creative effort.
Franklin D. Roosevelt
1933

Without regard to party, the overwhelming majority of our people seek a greater opportunity for humanity to prosper and find happiness.
Franklin D. Roosevelt
1934

HUMAN RIGHTS

The ideals of this country are the best of any country on the face of the Earth, but they have not been applied equally to all. We must take specific steps to include those who have been excluded, whether from govern-ment itself or from the opportunity to succeed in a free society.
George Bush
1988

If we in the United States are not strong enough, not courageous enough to stand up for human rights, who will?
George Bush
1988

A bill of rights is what the people are entitled to against every government on earth.
Thomas Jefferson
1787

No man has a natural right to commit aggression on the equal rights of another.
Thomas Jefferson
1816

There are certain rights possessed by each individual American citizen ... He claims them because he is himself a man, fashioned by the same Almighty hand as the rest of his species.
William Henry Harrison
1841

There are certain individual rights possessed by each individual American citizen which in his compact with the others he has never surrendered.
William Henry Harrison
1841

The man who holds that every human right is secondary to his profit must now give way to the advocate of human welfare.
Theodore Roosevelt
1910

What I am interested in is having the Government of the United States more concerned about human rights than property rights. Property is an instrument of humanity; humanity isn't an instrument of property.
Woodrow Wilson
1912

It is not property but the right to hold property, both great and small, which our Constitution guaranteed.
Calvin Coolidge
1925

At the heart of our American system is ... the ideal that there shall be an opportunity in life, an equal opportunity ... It holds that ... [all] ... have the chance to rise to any position which their character and ability may entitle them.
Herbert Hoover
1936

The first half of the century has been marked by
unprecedented and brutal attacks on the rights of man,
and by the two most frightful wars in history. The supreme need of our time is for man to learn to live together
in peace and harmony.
Harry S Truman
1949

We believe that all men are created equal because they
are created in the image of God.
Harry S Truman
1949

I emphasize the ... importance ... of the point dealing
with the declaration on human rights. I felt very strongly
about the need for a world "bill of rights" something on
the order of our own.
Harry S Truman
1955

Our civil and social rights form a central part of the
heritage we are striving to defend on all fronts and with
all our strength.
Dwight D. Eisenhower
1953

Although our civil liberties also serve important
private purposes—above all they were considered essential to the republican form of government. Such a government required that the consent of the governed be given
freely, thoughtfully and intelligently. Without freedom of
speech, freedom of assembly, freedom of religion, freedom
of the press, equal protection of the laws, and other unal-
ienable rights, men could not govern themselves intelligently.
John F. Kennedy
1959

The Universal Declaration of Human Rights guides
our actions ... to ease the plight of those whose basic
rights have been denied.
  Richard Nixon
  1973

We became an independent nation in a struggle for
human rights, and there have been many such struggles
since then—for the abolition of slavery, for universal
suffrage, for racial equality, for the rights of workers, for
women's rights. Not all of these struggles have yet been
won, but the freedom and vigor of our national public life
is evidence of the rights and the liberties we have
achieved.
  Jimmy Carter
  1977

Strengthened international machinery will help us to
close the gap between promise and performance in pro-
tecting human rights. ... The solemn commitment of the
United Nations Charter, of the United Nations Universal
Declaration for Human Rights, of the Helsinki Accords ...
must be taken just as seriously as commercial or security
commitments.
  Jimmy Carter
  1977

We have no wish to tell other nations what political or
social system they should have, but we want our own
worldwide influence to reduce human suffering and not
to increase it. We are therefore working to advance a
whole range of human rights—economic and social as
well as political.
  Jimmy Carter
  1977

We measure the real meaning of America in our
intangible values—values which do not change: our care

for each other, our commitment to freedom, our search for justice, our devotion to human rights and to world peace, and the patriotism and basic goodness of our people.

Jimmy Carter
1979

Our security is tied to human rights and social justice prevailing among other people on earth.

Jimmy Carter
1980

Never is there any excuse for the violation of the fundamental rights of man—not at any time or in any place, not in rich countries or poor, not under any social, economic or political system.

Ronald Reagan
1981

It was the Pope, at the end of World War II, when the world was so devastated, and yet we alone remained so strong, who said: "America has a genius for great and unselfish deeds, and into the hands of America, God has placed an afflicted mankind." I think that was a trust given to us that we should never betray. It is this responsibility as a free people that we face today.

Ronald Reagan
1981

Human rights are rights of individuals: rights of conscience, rights of choice, rights of association, rights of emigration, rights of self-directed action, and the right to own property. The concept of a nation of free men and women linked together voluntarily is the genius of the system that our Founding Fathers established. We will continue to strive to respect these rights fully in our own country and to promote their observance abroad.

Ronald Reagan
1981

POVERTY

Poverty remains a serious problem ... , especially for the very old, women living alone, and for minorities.
George Bush
1988

I find myself haunted by the lives being lived by the children of our inner cities. Children growing up, some of them, in a loveless environment, growing up amidst horror and violence.
George Bush
1988

What are some of the things that can be done? ... I want our affluent to help our poor. And I want our young to help our elderly ... I want the young men and women of our ... suburbs to get on a bus, or the subway, or the metro, and go into the cities where the want is ... The Peace Corps ... takes volunteers out of their lives and puts them in another place, another country. I want this sense of involvement and altruism to be local, personal and integrated into our young people's lives.
George Bush
1988

As a nation we must prevent hunger and cold to those of our people who are in honest difficulties.
Herbert Hoover
1930

The lessons of history, confirmed by the evidence immediately before me show conclusively that continued dependence upon relief induces a spiritual and moral disintegration fundamentally destructive to the national fibre. To dole out relief in this way is to administer a narcotic, a subtle destroyer of the human spirit. It is inimical to the dictates of sound policy. It is in violation of

the traditions of America. Work must be found for able-
bodied but destitute workers. The Federal Government
must and shall quit this business of relief.
Franklin D. Roosevelt
1935

In this nation I see tens of millions of its citizens ...
denied the greater part of what the very lowest standards
of today call the necessities of life ... I see one-third of a
nation ill-housed, ill-clad, ill-nourished. ... The Nation,
seeing and understanding the injustice of it, proposes to
paint it out.
Franklin D. Roosevelt
1937

The hopes of the Republic cannot forever tolerate
either undeserved poverty or self-serving wealth.
Franklin D. Roosevelt
1941

The American people have decided that poverty is just
as wasteful and just as unnecessary as preventable dis-
ease. We have pledged our common resources to help one
another in the hazards and struggles of individual life.
Harry S Truman
1949

Only by helping the least fortunate of its members to
help themselves can the human family achieve the decent,
satisfying life that is the right of all people.
Harry S Truman
1949

In a modern industrial society, banishment of destitution and cushioning the shock of personal disaster on the
individual are proper concerns of all levels of government,
including the Federal government.
Dwight D. Eisenhower
1954

From the deserts of North Africa to the islands of the South Pacific, one-third of all mankind has entered upon an historic struggle for a new freedom; freedom from grinding poverty.
Dwight D. Eisenhower
1957

The war against poverty will not be won here in Washington. It must be won in the field—in every private home, in every public office from the courthouse to the White House.
Lyndon B. Johnson
1964

Our aim is not to relieve the symptoms of poverty but to cure it.
Lyndon B. Johnson
1964

The cause of poverty may lie deeper—in our failure to give our fellow citizens a fair chance to develop their own capacities—in a lack of education and training, in a lack of medical care and housing, in a lack of decent communities to live and bring up their children.
Lyndon B. Johnson
1964

Our chief weapons in a more pinpointed attack will be better schools, and better health, and better homes, and better training, and better job opportunities to help more Americans—especially young Americans—escape from poverty, squalor and misery and unemployment rolls where other citizens help to carry them.
Lyndon B. Johnson
1964

The war on poverty ... began when this country began. It's been the most successful war on poverty in the

history of nations. There's more wealth in America today, more broadly shared, than in any nation in the world.
  Richard Nixon
  1968

Government has an important role in helping develop a country's economic foundation. But the critical test is whether government is genuinely working to liberate individuals, by creating incentives to work, save, invest and succeed ... Individual farmers, laborers, owners, traders and managers—they are the heart and soul of development ... Whenever they are allowed to create and build, ... societies become more dynamic, prosperous, progressive and free.
  Ronald Reagan
  1981

PUBLIC OPINION

In proportion as the structure of a government gives force to public opinion, it is essential that public opinion should be enlightened.
  George Washington
  1796

Public opinion sets the bounds to every government, and is the real sovereign in every free one.
  James Madison
  1791

Public opinion in this country is all-powerful.
  James Buchanan
  1859

Our government rests in public opinion. Whoever can change public opinion can change the government.
  Abraham Lincoln
  1856

He who molds public sentiment goes deeper than he who enacts statutes or pronounces decisions. He makes statutes or decisions possible or impossible.
Abraham Lincoln
1858

Public sentiment is everything. With public sentiment nothing can fail; without it nothing can succeed.
Abraham Lincoln
1858

Opinion is the great, indeed the only coordinating force in our system.
Woodrow Wilson
1908

A government can be no better than the public opinion which sustains it.
Franklin D. Roosevelt
1936

PUBLIC/PRIVATE PARTNERSHIPS

I have spoken, in the past, of a thousand points of light. I was using the phrase as shorthand for the fact that we are a nation of communities, of thousands of businesses and professional and religious and ethnic and regional communities and in this diversity and pluralism is our salvation. That's where America will be saved — in our communities, which are spread like stars, like a thousand points of light in a broad and peaceful sky. ... In a national movement such as "Yes To America" I am saying, "Add your light to the sum of light. Give to those who cross your path and enter your life ... Love your country and make your love real by a new engagement in the lives of your countrymen."
George Bush
1988

From now on in America, any definition of a successful life must include serving others.
George Bush
1988

We are a partnership or nothing.
Woodrow Wilson
1919

Progress is born of cooperation in the community—not from governmental restraints.
Herbert Hoover
1929

In the face of widespread hardship our people have demonstrated daily a magnificent sense of humanity, of individual and community responsibility for the welfare of the less fortunate. They have grown in their conceptions and organization for cooperative action for the common welfare.
Herbert Hoover
1932

Such people in need in the days before the great depression were cared for by local efforts—by States, by counties, by towns, by cities, by churches, and by private welfare agencies. It is my thought that in the future they must be cared for as they were before.
Franklin D. Roosevelt
1935

The Nation must ... treat resource development as a partnership undertaking— partnership in which the participation of private citizens and State and local governments is as necessary as is Federal participation.
Dwight D. Eisenhower
1955

And so, my fellow Americans, ask not what your
country can do for you; ask what you can do for your
country.
>   *John F. Kennedy*
>   *1961*

Only a total working partnership among Federal, State
and local governments can succeed. The test ... will be the
concern of each public institution, each private institution
and each responsible citizen.
>   *Lyndon B. Johnson*
>   *1967*

A new volunteer movement ... will not come out of
Washington, replete with slogans and catchy labels. It will
come from the people, from the grassroots.
>   *Richard Nixon*
>   *1968*

One of the great, distinguishing characteristics of the
American people is their readiness to join together in
helping one another. ... Today ... more than ever, America
needs the enlistment of the energies and resources of its
people, not as substitutes for government action, but as
supplements to it.
>   *Richard Nixon*
>   *1969*

The Office of Voluntary Action ... will help expand
and multiply innovative voluntary action programs ...
Representatives of States and local government will also
be consulted ... A creative partnership is possible.
>   *Richard Nixon*
>   *1969*

The genius of America has been its incredible ability to
improve the lives of its citizens through a unique combination of governmental and free citizen activity.
>   *Gerald R. Ford*
>   *1976*

Successful problem-solving requires more than Federal action alone; ... it involves a full partnership among all branches and all levels of government, and public policies which nurture and promote the creative energies of private enterprises, institutions and individual citizens.
Gerald R. Ford
1977

Each of us must rededicate ourselves to serving the common good. We are a community. Our individual fates are linked; our futures intertwined; and if we act in that knowledge and in that spirit together, as the Bible says: "We can move mountains."
Jimmy Carter
1978

We're asking you to encourage greater contributions of voluntary and personal involvement to form a partnership between the private and public sector for the good of America.
Ronald Reagan
1981

The success story of America is neighbor helping neighbor.
Ronald Reagan
1981

AREAS OF TRIAL

ARMS CONTROL/DISARMAMENT

My fourth proposal—actually a set of proposals—
concerns a less militarized Europe, the most heavily
armed continent in the world. Nowhere is this more
important than in the two Germanys. And that's why
our quest to safely reduce armaments has a special
significance for the German people.

To those who are impatient with our measured pace
in arms reductions, I respectfully suggest that history
teaches us a lesson—that unity and strength are the
catalyst and prerequisite to arms control. We've always
believed that a strong Western defense is the best road to
peace. Forty years of experience have proven us right.
  George Bush
  1989

Disarmament can never be of prime importance; there
is more need to get rid of the causes of war than of the
implements of war.
  Theodore Roosevelt
  1905

I have made it clear that ... we stand ready to cooper-
ate at any time in practicable measures on a world-wide
basis looking to immediate reduction of armaments.
  Franklin D. Roosevelt
  1934

We confront the issue of disarmament. On that issue
our policy is clear ... First we propose to press, continu-
ally, for a limitation of armaments by international agreement. Second, failing to get that, we will make no increase
of our own armaments unless other powers, by increasing
their armaments, make increase by us necessary to our
national safety.
  Franklin D. Roosevelt
  1936

The national debt of almost all nations would be far lower today if competitive armaments had not existed in the last quarter of a century.
Franklin D. Roosevelt
1941

We stand ready to engage with any and all others in joint efforts to remove the cause of mutual fear and distrust among nations, so as to make possible drastic reductions of armaments.
Dwight D. Eisenhower
1953

Disarmament programs are manifestly critical and complex. Neither the United States nor any other nation can properly claim to possess a perfect ... formula. ... But the formula matters less than ... the good faith without which no formula can work.
Dwight D. Eisenhower
1953

You can be sure that our government will continue its efforts in behalf of effective control and reduction of all armaments.
Dwight D. Eisenhower
1957

Men no longer pretend that the quest for disarmament is a sign of weakness—for in the spiraling arms race, a nation's security may well be shrinking even as its arms increase ... To destroy arms, however, is not enough. We must create even as we destroy—creating world-wide law and law enforcement as we outlaw world-wide war and weapons.
John F. Kennedy
1963

The United States a decade ago was instrumental in establishing a representative international forum for examination of arms control ... Advances in arms control have enhanced prospects for a new era of mutual security in the world.
Richard Nixon
1972

The arms race is now embedded in the very fabric of international affairs. ... Poverty and inequality are of such monumental scope that it will take decades of deliberate and determined effort ... to improve the situation substantially.
Jimmy Carter
1977

The United States has been preparing carefully for resumption of strategic arms negotiations ... based on substantial militarily significant reduction in forces, equal ceilings for similar types of forces, and adequate provisions for verification.
Ronald Reagan
1981

A year ago I said the time was right to move forward on arms control. I ... said nothing would have a higher priority in this Administration ... The prevention of conflict and the reduction of weapons are the most important public issues of our time.
Ronald Reagan
1982

FREEDOM OF EXPRESSION/THE MEDIA

The abuses of the press are notorious.
John Adams
1775

Our freedom depends upon the freedom of the press.
Thomas Jefferson
1787

Were it left to me to decide whether we should have a government without newspapers, or newspapers without a government, I should not hesitate a moment to choose the latter.
Thomas Jefferson
1787

To the press alone, chequered as it is with abuses, the world is indebted for all the triumphs which have been gained by reason and humanity over error and oppression.
Thomas Jefferson
1800

They [newspapers] live by the zeal they can kindle, and the schisms they can create. It is a contest of opinion ... which makes us take great interest in them.
Thomas Jefferson
1801

During the course of this administration, and in order to disturb it, the artillery of the press has been leveled against us, charged with whatsoever licentiousness could devise or dare. These abuses of an institution so important to freedom and science are deeply to be regretted.
Thomas Jefferson
1805

The press, confined to the truth, needs no other legal restraint; the public judgement will correct false reasonings and opinions on a full hearing of all parties.
Thomas Jefferson
1805

Where the press is free, and every man able to read, all is safe.
> *Thomas Jefferson*
> *1816*

The press is the best instrument for enlightening the mind of man and improving him as a rational, moral and social being.
> *Thomas Jefferson*
> *1823*

To answer newspaper accusations would be an endless task ... I have not the time to spare.
> *John Quincy Adams*
> *1821*

The maxim which our ancestors derived from the mother country that "freedom of the press is the great bulwark of civil and religious liberty" is one of the most precious legacies which they have left us.
> *William Henry Harrison*
> *1841*

I would honor the man who gave his country a good newspaper.
> *Rutherford B. Hayes*
> *1881*

We have all of us at times suffered from the liberties of the press, but we have to take the good and the bad.
> *Theodore Roosevelt*
> *1883*

I am going to do what I think is best for the country. The misrepresentations which are made by the muckraking correspondents I cannot neutralize, and don't intend to.
> *William H. Taft*
> *1910*

Absolute freedom of the press to discuss public questions is a foundation stone of American liberty.
Herbert Hoover
1929

Freedom of conscience, of education, of speech, of assembly are among the very fundamentals of democracy and all of them would be nullified should freedom of the press ever be successfully challenged.
Franklin D. Roosevelt
1940

The President of a great democracy such as ours, and the editors of great newspapers such as yours, owe a common obligation to the people: An obligation to present the facts, to present them with candor, and to present them in perspective.
John F. Kennedy
1961

The American press prints a lot of bad news, because bad news is news and good news is not news.
John F. Kennedy
1962

I sometimes think we are too much impressed by the clamor of daily events. Newspaper headlines and the television screens give us a short view ... It is the great moments of history, and not the passing excitements, that will shape our future.
John F. Kennedy
1963

INFLATION

This high inflation drained the earnings of working men and women, and sapped the strength of our economy. In particular, inflation hurt those who live on a fixed income: seniors and low-income Americans.
George Bush
1988

Prophets of doom predicted that the United States could not escape a runaway inflation during the war and an economic collapse after the war. These predictions have not been borne out.
Harry S Truman
1946

If we take the right steps in time we can certainly avoid the disastrous excesses of runaway booms and headlong depressions. We must not let a year or two of prosperity lull us into a false feeling of security and a repetition of the 1920s that culminated in the crash of 1929.
Harry S Truman
1946

We can control inflation if we make up our minds to do it.
Harry S Truman
1946

A balanced budget is an essential first measure in checking further depreciation in the buying power of the dollar.
Dwight D. Eisenhower
1953

The damaging effect of inflation on the wages, pensions, salaries and savings of us all has been brought under control.
Dwight D. Eisenhower
1953

The principal threat to efficient functioning of the free enterprise system is inflation.
Dwight D. Eisenhower
1956

We must encourage the self-discipline, the restraint necessary to curb the wage price spiral.
Dwight D. Eisenhower
1959

We must fight inflation as we would fight a fire that imperils our home.
Dwight D. Eisenhower
1959

History makes clear the risks inherent in any failure to deal firmly with the basic causes of inflation ... It [inflation] deals most cruelly with those who can least protect themselves.
Dwight D. Eisenhower
1959

Under the present Administration ... [President Eisenhower] ... it [inflation] ... has been regarded as the supreme threat. I would consider there were other threats—in space, in the tremendously increasing military superiority of the Soviet Union. These are all threats ... So we have to make a judgment between alternative forces.
John F. Kennedy
1959

Recession is only one enemy of a free economy—inflation is another. Inflation too often follows in the shadow of growth—while price stability is made easy by stagnation or controls.
John F. Kennedy
1962

A stronger nation and economy require more than a balanced budget. They require progress in those programs that spur our growth and fortify our strength.
John F. Kennedy
1962

It is tempting to blame someone else for inflation. Some blame business for raising prices and some blame unions for asking for more wages. But a review of the stark fiscal facts of the 1960s clearly demonstrates ... the Federal Government spent $57 billion more than it took in in taxes. ... Now millions of Americans are forced to go into debt today because the Federal Government decided to go into debt yesterday.
Richard Nixon
1970

Working together we will break the back of inflation— and we will do it without the mandatory wage and price controls that crush economic and personal freedom.
Richard Nixon
1972

Inflation, at the current, unacceptably high levels, is the direct result of economic problems that have been building, virtually without let up, for over a decade. There are no easy answers ... We know we cannot spend our way out of this problem.
Jimmy Carter
1981

Inflation today is caused by government simply spend- ing more than government takes in at the same time that government has imposed upon business and industry ... harassing regulations and punitive taxes that have reduced productivity. ... When you are reducing productivity at the same time that you are turning out printing-press money in excessive amounts, you're causing inflation.
Ronald Reagan
1980

We know only that inflation results from ... deficit spending. Government has only two ways of getting money, other than raising taxes. It can go into the money market and borrow, competing with its own citizens and driving up the interest rates, which it has done, or it can print money, and it's done that. Both methods are inflationary.
> *Ronald Reagan*
> *1981*

MILITARY DRAFT

Had we formed a permanent army in the beginning ... we should never have had to retreat with a handful of men across the Delaware in Seventy-six.
> *George Washington*
> *1780*

To be prepared for war is one of the most effectual ways of preserving the peace ... A free people ought not only be armed, but disciplined; to which end a uniform and well-digested plan is requisite.
> *George Washington*
> *1790*

Every citizen ... [should] ... be a soldier. This was the case with the Greeks and the Romans, and must be that of every free state.
> *Thomas Jefferson*
> *1813*

Our standing army is to be found in the bosom of society. It is composed of free citizens, who are ever ready to take up arms in the service of their country when an emergency requires it.
> *James K. Polk*
> *1848*

The principle of the draft ... is not new. It has been
practiced in all ages of the world ... It has been used ... in
establishing our independence, and it was also used under
the Constitution in 1812.
Abraham Lincoln
1863

I am distinctly in favor of a selective training bill and I
consider it necessary to the national defense.
Franklin D. Roosevelt
1940

America has adopted selective service in time of peace
and, in doing so, has broadened and enriched our basic
concept of citizenship. Universal service will bring not
only greater preparedness to meet the threat of war, but a
wider distribution of tolerance and understandings to
enjoy the blessings of peace.
Franklin D. Roosevelt
1940

The backbone of our military should be the trained
citizen ... who becomes a soldier or a sailor only in time of
danger. ... We can meet the need of a trained reserve in
one way—by universal training.
Harry S Truman
1955

From the beginning of my administration in 1945, I
had publicly favored a program of military training for
boys and young men. At a press conference on August 16
I was asked if I would propose peacetime conscription. I
replied that I would ask Congress to enact a program of
universal training for American youth.
Harry S Truman
1945

President Washington instituted the first military policy of the United States when he recommended universal draft as a guarantee of basic minimum protection for the Republic against aggressors. Washington's policy was not implemented until 1917 when President Wilson authorized the first compulsory draft ... During the nation's other great crisis in the 1860s, the lack of a firm military policy resulted in disgraceful draft riots and mob actions.
   Harry S Truman
   1955

We are now moving to a volunteer armed force. In order for that volunteer armed force to be adequately served, ... we are going to have to give respect to those that guard the United States in times of peace.
   Richard Nixon
   1972

This morning I'll be signing a proclamation to implement the terms of the registration act that the Congress recently passed ... The registration act ... is not to threaten war, but is to preserve peace.
   Jimmy Carter
   1980

We do not anticipate departing from a full-volunteer military force ... We are registering today just in case we are challenged in the future ... That's the best way to make sure that we will be strong.
   Jimmy Carter
   1980

I am opposed to a peacetime draft ... I am happy to tell you today that the enlistments [in the volunteer Armed Services] are up ... The education and quality level of the men enlisting is higher than it has ever been.
   Ronald Reagan
   1981

Even though we have a registration and I am convinced that it is worth keeping, I am opposed to a peacetime draft ... because we don't need it.
Ronald Reagan
1982

RELIGION/CHURCH AND STATE

People have asked me what it was that sustained me as I floated—alone—in that life raft, hoping that I might be rescued by a friendly ship. The answer is the same things that sustain me now, as I undertake this most important mission of my life: strength drawn from family, belief in God, and an unwavering faith in the United States of America.
George Bush
1988

The propitious smiles of Heaven can never be expected on a nation that disregards the eternal rules of order and right which heaven itself has ordained.
George Washington
1789

No people can be bound to acknowledge ... the Invisible Hand which conducts the affairs of men more than those of the United States. Every step by which they have advanced to the character of an independent nation seems to have been distinguished by some form of providential agency.
George Washington
1789

The Government of the United States ... gives to bigotry no sanction, to persecution no assistance.
George Washington
1790

I am for freedom of religion against all maneuvers to bring about a legal ascendency of one sect over another.
Thomas Jefferson
1799

I never will, by any word or act, bow to the shrine of intolerance, or admit a right of inquiry into the religious opinions of others. On the contrary, we are bound, you, I and everyone, to make common cause, even with error itself, to maintain the common right of freedom of conscience.
Thomas Jefferson
1803

Being a humble instrument in the hands of our Heavenly Father, as I am ... have desired that all my works and acts may be according to His will.
Abraham Lincoln
1862

Leave the matter of religion to the family altar, the church and the private school ... Keep the church and State forever separate.
Ulysses S. Grant
1875

Where freedom of religion has been attacked, the attack has come from sources opposed to democracy. Where democracy has been overthrown, the spirit of free worship has disappeared. And where religion and democracy have vanished, good faith and reason in international affairs have given way to strident ambition and brute force.
Franklin D. Roosevelt
1939

An ordering of society which relegates religion, democracy, and good faith among nations to the background can find no place within it for the ideals of the Prince of Peace. The United States rejects such an ordering and retains its ancient faith.

Franklin D. Roosevelt
1939

Peace on earth, good-will toward men—democracy must cling to that message.

Franklin D. Roosevelt
1944

We need to remember that the separation of church and state must never mean the separation of religious values from the lives of public servants.

Lyndon B. Johnson
1961

TAXES

There is no reason why the government has to take an ever increasing share of our resources. Americans are not under taxed. Taxes are about 19.4 percent of GNP, close to the record for the past 40 years ... But spending is 23 percent of GNP. So let's not fool ourselves. We've got to work the deficit down the old-fashioned way, by controlling government spending.

George Bush
1988

There's no quicker way to kill prosperity than to raise taxes.

George Bush
1988

[A] ... means of silently lessening the inequality of property is to exempt all from taxation below a certain point, and to tax the higher portions of property in geometric progression as they rise ...
Thomas Jefferson
1785

Care should be taken that it ... [taxation] ... be done in a manner not to benefit the wealthy few at the expense of the toiling millions ...
James K. Polk
1845

The burdens of government should as far as practicable be distributed justly and equally among all classes of our population.
James K. Polk
1845

I believe in a graduated income tax on big fortunes.
Theodore Roosevelt
1910

The collection of any taxes which are not absolutely required ... [for] ... the public welfare is only a species of legalized larceny.
Calvin Coolidge
1925

Taxes, after all, are the dues we pay for the privileges of membership in an organized society.
Franklin D. Roosevelt
1936

While we are moving toward lower levels of taxation, we must thoroughly revise our whole tax system.
Dwight D. Eisenhower
1954

We must revise our tax system both to ease the burden of heavy taxation and to encourage the investment necessary for the creation of jobs for all Americans who want to work.
Gerald R. Ford
1977

The taxing power … must not be used to regulate the economy or bring about social change.
Ronald Reagan
1981

WAR

My generation has lived in the shadows of war—World War II and the Cold War. We have lived partly in the sunlight but always in the shadow of struggle … That struggle … is not yet over.
George Bush
1988

A strong America, allied to other strong democracies, is the best insurance policy against war.
George Bush
1988

In the whole animal kingdom I recollect no animal but man, steadily and systematically employed in the destruction of itself.
Thomas Jefferson
1791

My feeling is in favor of the abolition of war ... by improving the mind and morals of society ... but of its abolition I despair.
Thomas Jefferson
1817

My life has been devoted to arms, yet I look upon war as a national calamity.
Zachary Taylor
1848

Both parties deprecate war, but now one of them would make war rather than let the nation survive, and the other would accept war than let it perish, and the war came.
Abraham Lincoln
1865

We entered this war [World War I] because violations of right had occurred which touched us ... and made the life of our own people impossible unless they were corrected ...
Woodrow Wilson
1917

The world has grown so small and the weapons of attack so swift that no nation can be safe so long as any other single powerful nation refuses to settle its grievances at the council table.
Franklin D. Roosevelt
1939

We have learned ... the old, old lesson that probability of attack is mightily decreased by the assurance of an ever ready defense.
Franklin D. Roosevelt
1939

Modern man can no longer live a civilized life if we are to go back to the practice of wars and conquests of the seventeenth and eighteenth centuries.
Franklin D. Roosevelt
1940

Exactly one year ago I said to this Congress: When the dictators are ready to make war upon us, they will not wait for an act of war on our part. ... They—not we—will choose the time and the place and the method of their attack ... We now know their choice of the time. A peaceful Sunday morning—December 7, 1941.
Franklin D. Roosevelt
1942

A soldier's pack is not so heavy a burden as a prisoner's chains.
Dwight D. Eisenhower
1953

War is the deadly harvest of arrogant and unreasoning minds.
Dwight D. Eisenhower
1957

The primary purpose of our arms is peace, not war. ... Our preparation against danger is our hope of safety.
John F. Kennedy
1961

Only when our arms are sufficient beyond doubt can
we be certain beyond doubt that they will never be employed.
    John F. Kennedy
    1961

Aggressive conduct, if allowed to go unchecked and
unchallenged, ultimately leads to war.
    John F. Kennedy
    1962

This nation's military objective has always been to
maintain peace by preventing war.
    Ronald Reagan
    1982

PEACE/NATIONAL DEFENSE

**We know, though some would like to forget, that
both peace and freedom depend on American strength
and American wisdom.**
    George Bush
    1988

**Many share the vision of peace with freedom, but
not all know how to achieve it ... When we have kept to
the principles of realism and strength, dialogue and
engagement, we have succeeded in advancing both
peace and freedom.**
    George Bush
    1988

To be prepared for war is one of the most effectual
means of preserving peace.
    George Washington
    1790

Even at this late hour, when our power to punish them [Whiskey Rebellion] can not be questioned, we shall not be unwilling to cement a lasting peace upon terms of candor, equity and good neighborhood.
George Washington
1794

With malice toward none, with charity toward all, with firmness in the right as God gives us to see the right, let us strive on to finish the work we are in, to bind the nation's wounds, to care for him who shall have borne the battle and for his widow and orphan, to do all which may achieve and cherish a just and lasting peace among ourselves and with all nations.
Abraham Lincoln
1865

I trust that the time is nigh when ... all international differences shall be determined ... by the ... processes of arbitration.
Chester A. Arthur
1882

The divergent interests of peace ... demanded a "more perfect union."
Benjamin Harrison
1889

Arbitration is the true method of settlement of international as well as of local or individual differences.
William McKinley
1898

There must not be a balance of power, but a community of power; not organized rivalries, but an organized common peace ...
Woodrow Wilson
1917

We are against war because it is destructive. We are for peace because it is constructive.
Calvin Coolidge
1924

After the First World War we tried to achieve a formula for permanent peace, based on magnificent idealism. We failed ... Today the United Nations can and must remain united for the maintenance of peace.
Franklin D. Roosevelt
1943

Our objective is to have a well-equipped, active defense force large enough—in concert with the forces of our allies—to deter aggression and to inflict punishing losses on the enemy immediately if we should be attacked.
Harry S Truman
1952

Warfare, no matter what weapons it employs, is a means to an end, and if that end can be achieved by negotiated settlements, ... there is no need for war.
Harry S Truman
1955

This ... [the Marshall Plan] ... was something new in the history of nations. The traditional practice had always been for the conqueror to strip the defeated countries to make off with whatever spoils were available. Our idea has been to restore the conquered nations ... to prosperity in the hope that they would understand the futility of aggression as a means of expansion and progress.
Harry S Truman
1955

The prudent man will not delude himself that his hope for peace guarantees the realization of peace. Even with genuine goodwill, time and effort will be needed to correct

the injustices that plague the earth today.
Dwight D. Eisenhower
1956

We must never become so preoccupied with our desire for military strength that we neglect those areas of economic development, trade diplomacy, education, ideas and principles where the foundation of real peace must be laid.
Dwight D. Eisenhower
1958

To achieve this peace we seek to prevent war at any place and in any dimension. If, despite our best efforts, a local dispute should flare into armed hostilities, the next problem would be to keep the conflict from spreading, and to compromising freedom. In support of these objectives, we maintain forces of great power and flexibility.
Dwight D. Eisenhower
1959

We look upon this shaken earth, and we declare our firm and fixed purpose—the building of a peace with justice in a world where moral law prevails.
John F. Kennedy
1961

Making peace is a tough, difficult, slow business— often much tougher and much slower than making war.
Lyndon B. Johnson
1968

Peace cannot be bought by ... wishful thinking or by slogans. It cannot be won by withdrawal ... Nor can it be achieved by ... nuclear weaponry.
Lyndon B. Johnson
1968

The greatest honor history can bestow is the title of
peacemaker.
Richard Nixon
1969

A global structure of peace requires a strong but
redefined American role ... [and] ... that other nations can
and should assume greater responsibility for their sake as
well as ours.
Richard Nixon
1969

The truest peace is based on self-restraint—on the
voluntary acceptance of those basic rules of behavior that
are rooted in mutual respect and demonstrated in mutual
forbearance.
Richard Nixon
1969

From its founding the Atlantic Alliance has preserved
the peace through unity, deterrence, and dialogue ...
These three elements of our policy have preserved peace
in Europe for more than a third of a century.
Ronald Reagan
1981

Peace is not the absence of conflict, but the ability to
cope with conflict by peaceful means.
Ronald Reagan
1982

CHALLENGES OF THE 1990s

DRUG ABUSE

Fundamentally, the drug problem in America is not one of supply, but of demand ... As long as Americans are willing to pay billions of dollars for illegal drugs, somebody somewhere in the world will provide them ... This fight will never be won by law enforcement alone; it will only be won by a change in public attitude, from tolerance to intolerance—of drug use and drug users.

George Bush
1988

CRIME

You're not going to solve the crime problem ... by talking tough while pursuing ... failed policies ... It's long past time that the federal death penalty be put back in use ... (that) judges do what they're supposed to do, ... and (there's) certainty in punishment ... We need to target the career criminal, ... (and) ... increase technical and financial assistance to local law enforcement ... Finally, we must attack two of the root causes of the culture of crime—illiteracy and drugs. We must help the first-time offender escape the culture of crime, before society loses him for good.

George Bush
1988

HOMELESSNESS

I have great compassion for those who are homeless and live on the margin of society. This is a diverse group ... A significant number ... are younger men between 18 and 25 years old and families seeking shelter—and about 1 in 5 homeless work full-part time ... There are 1.7 million buildings that can be rehabilitated for use by the homeless. We should implement aspects of that report ... We must do more to eliminate the causes of homelessness.
> *George Bush*
> *1988*

ENVIRONMENT

We are all passengers together on a boat that we have damaged—not with the cataclysm of war, but with the slow neglect of a vessel we thought was impervious to our abuse. In the last analysis, we all have a stake in maintaining the ecological health of the planet ... Nature was once the great enemy of Man. ... Now we find that we must protect her from ourselves. A better America is a cleaner America.
> *George Bush*
> *1988*

HEALTH CARE

We have three basic choices before us. We could ... rely on people to perceive the problem and to provide appropriately for their needs ... call on the government to take care of the problem and impose the taxes that would be required ... (or) ... use the government to educate people about the problem and encourage them to provide for themselves to the extent they can, and ... help ... those who truly need help.
> *George Bush*
> *1988*

THE WORLD

WORLD PERSPECTIVE

Five revolutionary changes ... are reshaping the
international landscape. First, the democratic revolution. Ten years ago, 25 percent of the people of Latin
America lived under democratic governments—today 90
percent do.

Second, ... the revolution of free enterprise. The
American model of low taxes and economic growth is
being adopted around the world. Concepts of political
democracy and market economies are being debated
from Budapest to Moscow, from Warsaw to Beijing.

Fourth, (the) revolution in arms reduction. For the
first time in history the United States and the Soviet
Union will completely eliminate an entire class of their
nuclear missiles. Fifth, (the) revolution in information
and communications. A single individual, sitting at (a)
desk-top computer, can access more resources of information world-wide than were recently available to the
most powerful governments.

All these revolutions present unparalleled opportunity—and risk. With the proper leadership America
should be able to direct these changes for the common
good.

> *George Bush*
> *1988*

The sacred model of liberty and the destiny of the
republican model of government are ... deeply and finally
staked on the experiment entrusted to the hands of the
American people.

> *George Washington*
> *1789*

We act not for ourselves alone but for the whole
human race. The event of our experiment is to show
whether man can be trusted with self-government.

> *Thomas Jefferson*
> *1802*

As American freemen we ... sympathize in all efforts to extend the blessings of civil and political liberty.
Zachary Taylor
1849

It is my firm conviction that the civilized world is tending toward ... government by the people ... and that our great Republic is destined to be the guiding star to all others.
Ulysses S. Grant
1873

I believe that our Great Maker is preparing the world, in His own good time, to become one nation, speaking one language, and when the armies and navies will be no longer required.
Ulysses S. Grant
1873

We have not sought to dominate or to absorb any of our weaker neighbors, but rather to aid and encourage them to establish free and stable governments resting upon the consent of their own people.
Benjamin Harrison
1889

The tragic events of the thirty months of virtual turmoil through which we have just passed ... [World War I] ... have made us citizens of the world. There can be no turning back now.
Woodrow Wilson
1917

An immortal sentence of Abraham Lincoln's—"Let us have faith that right makes might, and in that faith let us dare to do our duty as we understand it."
Woodrow Wilson
1920

Being a nation relying not on force, but on fair dealing and good will, to maintain peace with others, we have provided a modern military force in a form adapted solely to defense.

Calvin Coolidge
1927

In the field of world policy I would dedicate this nation to the policy of the good neighbor— ... the neighbor who respects his obligations and respects the sanctity of his agreements in and with a world of neighbors.

Franklin D. Roosevelt
The Good Neighbor Policy
1933

The people of other nations have the right to choose their own form of government. But we in this Nation believe that such a choice should be predicated on certain freedoms which we think are essential everywhere.

Franklin D. Roosevelt
1940

After the First World War we tried to achieve a formula for permanent peace based on a magnificent idealism. We failed. ... Today the United Nations are the mightiest military coalition in history ... The United Nations can and must remain united for the maintenance of peace.

Franklin D. Roosevelt
1943

In his last message on the State of the Union ... President Roosevelt said: "This new year of 1945 can be the greatest year of human achievement in human history" ... All these hopes and more were fulfilled in 1945 ... The plain fact is that civilization was saved in 1945 by the United Nations.

Harry S Truman
1946

We are convinced that the preservation of peace between nations requires a United Nations Organization composed of all the peace-loving nations of the world who are willing jointly to use force, if necessary, to insure peace.
>   *Harry S Truman*
>   *1946*

We are persuaded by necessity and by belief that the strength of all free peoples lies in unity; their danger in discord.
>   *Dwight D. Eisenhower*
>   *1953*

We must use our skills and knowledge and, at times, our substance, to help others rise from misery, however far the scene of suffering may be from our shores.
>   *Dwight D. Eisenhower*
>   *1957*

With both sections of this divided world in possession of unbelievably destructive weapons, mankind approaches a state where mutual annihilation becomes a possibility. No other fact of today's world equals this in importance—it colors everything we say, plan and do.
>   *Dwight D. Eisenhower*
>   *1960*

As a nation, we think not of war but of peace; not of crusades but of covenants of cooperation; not of pageantry or imperialism but of pride of new states freshly risen to independence.
>   *John F. Kennedy*
>   *1959*

Already the United Nations has become both the measure and the vehicle of man's most generous impulses.
>   *John F. Kennedy*
>   *1961*

Our basic goal remains the same: A peaceful world community of free and independent states—free to choose their own system, so long as it does not threaten the freedom of others.
John F. Kennedy
1962

The issue in the world struggle is … coercion versus free choice.
John F. Kennedy
1963

Marshall McLuhan says modern communications have turned the world into a global village. I would go beyond that. The world is becoming one great city … and as the rich and poor are brought closer together, the gap between them becomes sharper.
Richard Nixon
1967

Since World War II, the United States has moved into a new and unfamiliar position—often an uncomfortable position—of power and responsibility. We have inherited by default the role of the world's chief keeper of peace and guardian of freedom.
Richard Nixon
1968

We seek an open world—open to ideas, open to the exchange of goods and people, a world in which no people, great or small, will live in angry isolation.
Richard Nixon
1969

There are a number of lessons we can learn from Vietnam. One … is … that we have to learn to work with other governments that feel as we do that freedom is vitally important.
Gerald R. Ford
1975

The United States cannot solve the problems of the world. We can sometimes help others resolve their differences.
Jimmy Carter
1978

Our primary goal is to help shape a world which is more responsive to the desire of people everywhere for economic well-being, social justice, political self-determination and basic human rights.
Jimmy Carter
1978

We are witnessing today a great revolutionary crisis— a crisis where the demands of the economic order are colliding directly with those of the political order.
Ronald Reagan
1982

While we must be cautious about forcing the pace of change, we must not hesitate to declare our ultimate objectives and to take concrete actions to move toward them.
Ronald Reagan
1982

Our foreign policy, as President Eisenhower once said "is not difficult to state. We are for peace, first, last and always, for very simple reasons." We know that only in a peaceful atmosphere, a peace with justice, one in which we can be confident, can America prosper as we have known prosperity in the past.
Ronald Reagan
1982

Our commitment to self determination, freedom and peace is the very soul of America.
Ronald Reagan
1982

A LOOK AT OUR NEIGHBORS

AFRICA/ASIA

There is no region of the world in which the U.S. economic, political, and security interests are growing faster than East Asia and the Pacific Basin. Much of our future economic growth will be driven by trade and investment across the Pacific, which already surpasses trade and investment across the Atlantic. It is welcome news for the Americans that the dynamism and growth of this vital region is being fueled by market economies where democracy is on the march.

Yet we need to ensure that our trading partners open their markets more fairly to U.S. goods and services and to contribute more equitably to sharing the burdens of maintaining the security of the free world that has made their economic success possible.

George Bush
1988

The United States enjoys its best relations with both China and Japan since the days of Sun Yat-sen and the Treaty of Portsmouth in 1905. And our quiet diplomacy in South Korea seems to have nudged that country closer to full-fledged democracy.

George Bush
1988

The peoples of Asia want to be free to follow their own way of life. They want to preserve their cultures and their traditions ... just as ... we want to preserve ours. They are laboring under terrific handicaps of poverty, ill health, feudal systems of land ownership, and the threat of internal subversion and external attack. We can and must increase our help to them.

Harry S Truman
1952

Africa is undergoing an agricultural, technological, urban, social and political revolution. It is passing from a feudal—in some places still prehistoric—stage into the atomic age in a matter of decades. ... In the light of such fantastic variety and revolutionary progress, it is a mistake for the United States to fix its image of Africa in any single mold.
> *John F. Kennedy*
> *1959*

There is no single best way of life that answers the needs of everyone, everywhere ... What we do have in common with the free nations of Asia, Africa, Europe and Latin America are basic weighty convictions, more important than differences of speech and color and culture.
> *Dwight D. Eisenhower*
> *1960*

In Africa and Asia we are witnessing the turbulent unfolding of new nations and new continents ... We are committed to helping those governments dedicated to the welfare of their people. We seek not fidelity to an iron faith but diversity of belief as varied as man himself.
> *Lyndon B. Johnson*
> *1965*

In ... Asia the old barriers of indifference and rivalry are slowly being overcome—and a new spirit of cooperation is taking shape ... While our Asian friends still need a helping hand, they want to match it with their own efforts—aimed toward their own goals.
> *Lyndon B. Johnson*
> *1966*

CANADA

We have long had a close, even fraternal relationship with our neighbor, Canada, capped by a free trade agreement that I believe will rank as one of the most significant achievements of our administration.

George Bush
1988

We, the people of the United States and Canada are more than just good neighbors; we're good friends ... We each play a separate and important role in international affairs ... But these separate roles are respected by our two peoples and have never diminished the harmony between us.

Ronald Reagan
1981

CHINA (PEOPLE'S REPUBLIC OF CHINA)

Our relations with China are important in their own right, not in terms of what some have termed a 'card' in U.S.-Soviet relations. ... There's every reason our relations with China should grow and prosper in the years ahead because it is important to both our countries, strategically, culturally and economically.

George Bush
1988

We have begun a new chapter in American-Chinese relations. ... For two decades our two countries stared at each other icily across a gulf of hostility and suspicion. ... This situation has been transformed. ... Differences in ideology and policy remain, ... but ... the risk of confrontation ... has been sharply reduced.

Richard Nixon
1973

CUBA

Our determination to restore freedom and democracy to Cuba has never wavered and ... freedom there is not a bargaining chip of any kind at all.
George Bush
June 14, 1988

I candidly confess, that I have ever looked upon Cuba as the most interesting addition that could ever be made to our system of States. Yet, I have no hesitation in ... accepting its independence.
Thomas Jefferson
1823

We face at this moment a very important question—that of the future of relations between the United States and Cuba. ... Ever since the evacuation of the island by ... Spain, the executive ... has been assisting its people in the successive steps necessary to the establishment of a free and independent government.
William McKinley
1901

Our objection with Cuba is not over the people's drive for a better life. Our objection is to their domination by foreign and domestic tyrannies. Cuban social and economic reform should be encouraged.
John F. Kennedy
1961

Cuba became the first member of the American family to welcome into this hemisphere the armed power of a non-American state. That action created, among other things, the Cuban Missile Crisis of 1962.
Richard Nixon
1973

The Soviet brigade is a manifestation of Moscow's dominance of Cuba. It raises the level of responsibility that the Soviet Union must take for escalating Cuban military actions abroad.
Jimmy Carter
1979

Europe/NATO

NATO, under U.S. leadership, has been the most successful alliance in history. In 1989, we'll celebrate 40 years of keeping the peace ... I'll state my convictions simply. The survival of both peace and freedom will continue to depend on the Atlantic Alliance for the foreseeable future. There can be no substitute for the greatest coalition of free nations in history.
George Bush
1988

And let us be equal to the opportunity that lies before us. Let us have history write of us that we were the generation that made Europe whole and free.
George Bush
1989

A strong America, allied to other strong democracies ... is the best insurance policy against war.
George Bush
1988

Free Europe is entering into a new phase of its long and brilliant history. The era of colonial expansion has passed; the era of national rivalries is fading; and a new era of interdependence and unity is taking shape.
John F. Kennedy
1963

Twice in my lifetime, I have seen the peoples of Europe plunged into the tragedy of war ... And twice in my lifetime young Americans have bled their lives into the soil of those battlefields not to enrich our domain, but to restore the peace and independence of our friends and Allies. All of us who have lived through these times share a common resolve that they must never come again.
Ronald Reagan
1981

GREAT BRITAIN

Great Britain and the United States are kindred nations of like-minded people and must face their tests together. We are bound by common language and linked in history. We share laws and literature, blood and moral fibre. The responsibility for freedom is ours to share.
Ronald Reagan
1981

JAPAN

The Japanese-American relationship is the anchor of American policy in East Asia. It is a pillar of strength in a world where democratic values are always under challenge. Our friendship is based on respect and mutual trust.
Ronald Reagan
1981

LATIN AMERICA

Democracy is on a roll in Latin America. Since we took office, the following countries have changed from military to democratic rule: Argentina, Equador, Peru, Honduras, Grenada, El Salvador, Brazil, Uruguay and

Guatemala. Ninety percent of the population of Latin America now lives under democracy.
George Bush
1988

We share with Mexico a host of bilateral interests ... With a long and porous southern border, we must do whatever we can to bolster the strength of democracy and free enterprise in Mexico.
George Bush
1988

Let me turn first to Mexico. You cannot live in Texas as long as I have and not have a special feeling for our proud and fiercely independent neighbor to the south. The rapid growth of the Hispanic population and culture in the Southwest—indeed, even in my own family—has greatly enriched this melting pot called America.
I want to strive for ... a relationship of economic competition, strategic cooperation, and mutual trust, a relationship that recognizes our differences, yet moves us toward our common goals—greater prosperity and individual freedom.
George Bush
1988

I join in wishes for the emancipation of South America. That they will be liberated from foreign subjection I have little doubt.
Thomas Jefferson
1813

America, North and South, has a set of interests distinct from those of Europe ... She should therefore have a system of her own.
Thomas Jefferson
1823

The future is going to be very different in this hemisphere from the past. These States lying to the south of us, which have always been our neighbors, will now be drawn closer to us by innumerable ties, and, I hope, chief of all, by the tie of a common understanding of each other.
    Woodrow Wilson
    1913

In the field of world policy I would dedicate this nation to the policy of the good neighbor ... Throughout the Americas the spirit of the good neighbor is a practical and living fact.
    Franklin D. Roosevelt
    1936

One hundred and thirty nine years ago this week the United States, stirred by the heroic struggles of its fellow Americans, urged the independence and recognition of the new Latin American republics ... Our hemisphere's mission is not yet completed. For our unfulfilled task is to demonstrate to the entire world that man's unsatisfied aspiration for economic progress and social justice can best be achieved by free men working within the framework of democratic institutions.
    John F. Kennedy
    1961

We recognize that each nation's approach to development should reflect its own cultural, political and economic heritage. That is the way it should be. The great thing about our international system is that it respects diversity and promotes creativity. Certain economic factors, of course, apply across cultural and political lines. We are mutually interdependent, but, above all, we are individually responsible.
    Ronald Reagan
    1981

Our plans for the Caribbean Basin are one example of how we would like to harness economic energies within a region to promote stronger growth. The design and success of this undertaking depends upon the cooperation of many developed and developing countries.
Ronald Reagan
1981

Nearly a century ago, ... Jose Marti warned that "mankind is composed of two sorts of men—those who love and create, and those who hate and destroy." ... Today, more than ever, the compassionate, creative peoples of the Americas have an opportunity to stand together—to overcome injustice, hatred and oppression, and build a better life for all the Americas.
Ronald Reagan
1982

SOVIET UNION/RUSSIA

Soviet society today is clearly in the midst of dramatic change. There is a search for truth about the Soviet past, a willingness to challenge old dogmas, a pressure for economic reform ...
George Bush
1988

We welcome the developments in the Soviet Union— but we should not let our hopes outrun our practical experience ... We welcome what Mr. Gorbachev says—I am impressed by the steps he has taken for more openness, more reform, but the Soviet Union will be judged by what it delivers.
George Bush
1988

Forty years of perseverance have brought us a precious opportunity. And now, it is time to move beyond containment to a new policy for the 1990s—one that recognizes the full scope of change taking place around the world and in the Soviet Union itself.
George Bush
1989

Russia presents notable difficulties ... We have relieved their pitiable destitution with an enormous charity. ... Our government does not propose, however, to enter into relations with another regime which refuses to recognize the sanctity of international obligations.
Calvin Coolidge
1923

In the week of May 22-29, 1972, the United States and the Soviet Union took a decisive turn away from the confrontations of the past quarter-century. ... The agreement on twelve Basic Principles ... included ... avoid military confrontations ... exercise restraint in their mutual relations ... settle differences by peaceful means.
Richard Nixon
1973

We cannot expect the Soviet Union to show restraint in the face of ... United States weakness or irresolution.
Gerald R. Ford
1975

We invite the Soviet Union to consider with us now how the competition of ideas and values—which it is committed to support—can be conducted on a peaceful and reciprocal basis.
Ronald Reagan
1982

THE FUTURE

CHANGE

The revival of American leadership is today changing the world and shaping the future, creating new opportunities, new possibilities, barely dreamt of eight years ago.
George Bush
1988

Our leadership will reflect a strategic design that is different from that of our critics ... We will integrate every available policy instrument into a multifaceted approach. That means using negotiations, intelligence, economic strength and aid, public diplomacy, and, yes, military power.
George Bush
1988

I am dedicated to a new vision of a better America. It's a vision of hope for a safer and more peaceful world, of a gentler America, our values strong, a country richer for diversity. And it's a vision of more economic growth.
George Bush
1988

In the 1990s, we can move the world once again—or we can be pushed along by it.
George Bush
1988

For a new breeze is blowing, and a world refreshed by freedom seems reborn; for in man's heart, if not in fact, the day of the dictator is over. The totalitarian era is passing, its old ideas blown away like leaves from an ancient lifeless tree.
George Bush
1989

The theory of government changes with general progress.
>   *Ulysses S. Grant*
>   *1873*

Our duty may take many forms in the future ... We must ever face the fact of our shifting national needs.
>   *Theodore Roosevelt*
>   *1899*

Throughout the world change is the order of the day. In every nation economic problems ... have brought crises ... for which the masters of old practice and theory were unprepared.
>   *Franklin D. Roosevelt*
>   *1935*

Social justice ... has become a definite goal and ancient governments are beginning to heed the call. Thus, the American people do not stand alone in the world in their desire for change.
>   *Franklin D. Roosevelt*
>   *1935*

Throughout the world new ideas are challenging the old.
>   *Harry S Truman*
>   *1948*

The Second World War radically changed the power relationships of the world. Nations once great were left shattered and weak; channels of communication, routes of trade, political and economic ties of many kinds were ripped apart.
>   *Harry S Truman*
>   *1953*

There was another question posed for us at the war's
end, which ... concerned the future course of democracy:
Could the machinery of government and politics in this
Republic be changed, improved, adapted rapidly enough
... to carry ... through ... the vast new complicated under-
takings called for in our time?

We have answered this question ... with ... the reor-
ganization of Congress in 1946, the unification of our
armed services, beginning in 1947; the closer integration of
foreign and military policy through the National Security
Council created that same year; and the Executive reor-
ganizations, before and after the Hoover-Acheson Com-
mission report in 1949.

> *Harry S Truman*
> *1953*

Change is the inexorable law of life.

> *Dwight D. Eisenhower*
> *1953*

We now stand in the vestibule of a vast new technological age.

> *Dwight D. Eisenhower*
> *1959*

Even now a rocket moves toward Mars. It reminds us
the world will not be the same for our children, or even for
ourselves in a short span of years.

> *Lyndon B. Johnson*
> *1965*

Our destiny in the midst of change will rest on the
unchanged character of our people and on their faith.

> *Lyndon B. Johnson*
> *1965*

Never in human history have so many changes taken place in the space of one generation ... It is a world of new nations—it is a world of new people. Half the world's nations have been born since World War II ... It is a world of new ideas.
Richard Nixon
1967

The spiraling pace of change allows us to contemplate in our lifetime advances that once would have taken centuries.
Richard Nixon
1969

America, which has pioneered in the new abundance and in the new technology, is called upon today to pioneer in meeting the concerns which have followed in their wake.
Richard Nixon
1970

The era upon which we entered is not as easily defined as it is perceived ... The emergence of a post-industrial society is the dominant social reality of the present moment ... It is the fundamental thrust of technological change to change society as well. The fundamental task of government in the era now past was to somehow keep abreast of such change and respond to it. The task of government in the future will be to anticipate change, to prevent it where clearly nothing is to be gained; to prepare for it when on the balance the effects are to be desired; and above all, to build into the technology an increasing degree of understanding of its impact on human society.
Richard Nixon
1970

We live in a time of testing and a time of change.
Gerald R. Ford
1975

In less than a lifetime, world population has doubled
... Mass communications, literacy and migration ... have
awakened new yearnings for economic justice and human
rights. ... In such a world, the choice is ... between anarchy and destruction, cooperation and peace.
> *Jimmy Carter*
> *1979*

We need not fear change. The values on which our
nation was founded—individual liberty, self-determination, the potential for human fulfillment in freedom—all of
these endure.
> *Jimmy Carter*
> *1979*

Our history is one of a people diverse in backgrounds
but united in common values, facing one serious challenge
after another. We have faced depressions, wars, injustice,
and prevailed each time. We will prevail again, and, with
your help, meet fully the challenges of our time.
> *Jimmy Carter*
> *1980*

We live in a time of transition, an uneasy era which is
likely to endure for the rest of the century.
> *Jimmy Carter*
> *1981*

If there is a lesson for us, it is that we, as a free people,
must always be prepared for change so that when it
comes, we're ready to meet new challenges and opportunities. ... Our system of government is unique and best
able to change and to move forward without disruption or
break in continuity of purpose.
> *Ronald Reagan*
> *1982*

VISION OF THE FUTURE

The America I imagine, the America I will work for, is a nation of people who hail from all the nations of the world and who bring us their hopes and habits, each adding to the sum total of what we mean when we say "American."
George Bush
1988

The path of freedom leads to a larger home—a home where West meets East, a democratic home—the commonwealth of free nations.
George Bush
1989

Our time is a time of great hope and a time of enormous challenges. The new world we seek is shaped by an idea—an idea of universal appeal and undeniable force, and that idea is democracy.
George Bush
1989

Although I pretend no ... foresight into futurity, yet, ... as a philanthropist by character, and as a citizen of the great Republic at large, ... I consider how mankind may be connected like one great family in fraternal ties, ... that nations are becoming more humanized in their policy ... and, in fine, that the period is not very remote, when the benefits of a liberal and free commerce will pretty generally succeed to the devastations and horrors of war.
George Washington
1786

The struggle of today is not altogether for today—it is for a vast future, also.
Abraham Lincoln
1861

When there is no vision, the people perish.
Franklin D. Roosevelt
1933

I ask that all of us everywhere think things through with the single aim of how best to serve the future of our own Nation.
Franklin D. Roosevelt
1940

We stand at the opening of an era which can mean either great achievement or terrible catastrophe for ourselves and for all mankind.
Harry S Truman
1949

The American people desire, and are determined to work for, a world in which all nations and all peoples are free to govern themselves as they see fit and to achieve a decent and satisfying life.
Harry S Truman
1949

Since Alamagordo we have developed atomic weapons with many times the explosive force of the earlier models ... From now on man moves into a new era of destructive power.
Harry S Truman
1953

We stand today on the edge of a new frontier, a frontier of unknown opportunities and perils, a frontier of unfulfilled hopes and threats.
John F. Kennedy
1960

The road ahead, to be sure, is a hard road, a road that man has never traveled before, a road full of obstacles. But America has never long faltered in the face of new challenges.

John F. Kennedy
1960

We love our country most not for what it was, though it has always been great, not for what it is, though of this we are proud, but for what it can, through the efforts of us all, some day become.

John F. Kennedy
1961

We have undertaken ... a great new effort in outer space. ... Our objective is to develop in a new frontier of science, commerce and cooperation, the position of the United States and the free world.

John F. Kennedy
1962

Our ultimate goal is a world without war, a world made safe for diversity, in which all men, goods and ideas can move across every border and every boundary.

Lyndon B. Johnson
1964

Whether we shape the future in the image of our hopes is ours to determine by our actions and our choices.

Richard Nixon
1969

We share a bright vision of America's future—a vision of good life for all our people.

Jimmy Carter
1980

We who live in free market societies believe that growth, prosperity and, ultimately, human fulfillment are created from the bottom up, not the government down. Only when the human spirit is allowed to invent and create; only when individuals are given a personal stake in deciding economic policies and benefiting from their success—only then can societies remain economically alive, dynamic, prosperous, progressive and free.

Ronald Reagan
1981

THE PRESIDENTS

Please note: States listed are places of residence at time of election.
Wives listed are First Ladies during Presidents' terms of office.

George Washington

(No Party)

Profession: Farmer/Soldier
State: Virginia
Born: February 22, 1732
Died: December 14, 1799
Wife: Martha Custis
Religion: Episcopalian
Military: Commander-in-
   Chief, Continental Army

**1st President
(1789-1797)**

John Adams

Federalist

Profession: Lawyer
State: Massachusetts
Born: October 19, 1735
Died: July 4, 1826
Wife: Abigail Smith
Religion: Unitarian
Military: None

**2nd President
(1797-1801)**

Thomas Jefferson   Democratic-Republican

3rd President
(1801-1809)

Profession: Lawyer/Farmer
  Author/Inventor
State: Virginia
Born: April 13, 1743
Died: July 4, 1826
Wife: Martha Wayles Skelton
Religion: Deist
Military: Virginia Militia

James Madison   Democratic-Republican

4th President
(1809-1817)

Profession: Lawyer/Author
State: Virginia
Born: March 16, 1751
Died: June 28, 1836
Wife: Dolley Payne Todd
Religion: Episcopalian
Military: None

James Monroe   Democratic-Republican

Profession: Lawyer
State: Virginia
Born: April 28, 1758
Died: July 4, 1831
Wife: Elizabeth Kortright
Religion: Episcopalian
Military: Virginia Militia

5th President
(1817-1825)

John Quincy
Adams   Democratic-Republican

Profession: Lawyer
State: Massachusetts
Born: July 11, 1767
Died: February 23, 1848
Wife: Louisa Johnson
Religion: Unitarian
Military: None

6th President
(1825-1829)

Andrew Jackson

Democrat

Profession: Lawyer/Soldier
State: Tennessee
Born: March 15, 1767
Died: June 8, 1845
Wife: Rachel Robards
Religion: Presbyterian
Military: U.S. Army

7th President
(1829-1837)

Martin van Buren

Democrat

Profession: Lawyer
State: New York
Born: December 5, 1782
Died: July 24, 1862
Wife: Hannah Hoes
Religion: Dutch Reformed
Military: None

8th President
(1837-1841)

William Henry Harrison   **Whig**

Profession: Soldier
State: Ohio
Born: February 9, 1773
Died: April 4, 1841
Wife: Anna Symmes
Religion: Episcopalian
Military: U.S. Army

**9th President
(1841)**

John Tyler   **Whig**

Profession: Lawyer
State: Virginia
Born: March 29, 1790
Died: January 18, 1862
Wife: Letitia Christian
    (died 1842)
    Julia Gardner
    (married 1844)
Religion: Episcopalian
Military: U.S. Army

**10th President
(1841-1845)**

James Knox Polk

Democrat

11th President
(1845-1849)

Profession: Lawyer
State: Tennessee
Born: November 2, 1795
Died: June 15, 1849
Wife: Sarah Childress
Religion: Presbyterian
Military: None

Zachary Taylor

Whig

12th President
(1849-1850)

Profession: Farmer/Soldier
State: Louisiana
Born: November 24, 1784
Died: July 9, 1850
Wife: Margaret Smith
Religion: Episcopalian
Military: U.S. Army

Millard Fillmore   Whig

Profession: Lawyer
State: New York
Born: January 7, 1800
Died: March 8, 1874
Wife: Abigail Powers
Religion: Unitarian
Military: None

**13th President
(1850-1853)**

Franklin Pierce   Democrat

Profession: Lawyer
State: New Hampshire
Born: November 23, 1804
Died: October 8, 1869
Wife: Jane Means Appleton
Religion: Episcopalian
Military: U.S. Army

**14th President
(1853-1857)**

James Buchanan   Democrat

Profession: Lawyer
State: Pennsylvania
Born: April 23, 1791
Died: June 1, 1868
Wife: None
Religion: Presbyterian
Military: None

**15th President
(1857-1861)**

Abraham Lincoln   Republican

Profession: Lawyer
State: Illinois
Born: February 12, 1809
Died: April 15, 1865
Wife: Mary Todd
Religion: None formally
Military: U.S. Army

**16th President
(1861-1865)**

Andrew Johnson   Democrat*

17th President
(1865-1869)

Profession: Tailor
State: Tennessee
Born: December 29, 1808
Died: July 31, 1875
Wife: Eliza McCardle
Religion: None formally
Military: None

* entered office on National Union ticket

Ulysses Simpson Grant   Republican

18th President
(1869-1877)

Profession: Soldier/Farmer
State: Illinois
Born: April 27, 1822
Died: July 23, 1885
Wife: Julia Boggs Dent
Religion: Methodist
Military: U.S. Army

Rutherford Birchard Hayes   Republican

Profession: Lawyer/Soldier
State: Ohio
Born: October 4, 1822
Died: January 17, 1893
Wife: Lucy Ware Webb
Religion: Methodist
Military: U.S. Army

19th President
(1877-1881)

James Abram Garfield   Republican

Profession: Lawyer/Soldier
State: Ohio
Born: November 19, 1831
Died: September 19, 1881
Wife: Lucretia Rudolph
Religion: Disciples of Christ
Military: U.S. Army

20th President
(1881)

Chester Alan Arthur — Republican

Profession: Lawyer/Teacher
State: New York
Born: October 5, 1830
Died: November 18, 1886
Wife: Ellen Herndon
Religion: Episcopalian
Military: U.S. Army

**21st President
(1881-1885)**

Grover Cleveland — Democrat

Profession: Lawyer
State: New York
Born: March 18, 1837
Died: June 24, 1908
Wife: Francis Folsom
Religion: Presbyterian
Military: None

**22nd President
(1885-1889)
24th President
(1893-1897)**

Benjamin Harrison

Republican

23rd President
(1889-1893)

Profession: Lawyer/Soldier
State: Indiana
Born: August 20, 1833
Died: March 13, 1901
Wife: Caroline Scott
Religion: Presbyterian
Military: U.S. Army

William McKinley

Republican

25th President
(1897-1901)

Profession: Lawyer/Teacher
State: Ohio
Born: January 29, 1843
Died: September 14, 1901
Wife: Ida Saxton
Religion: Methodist
Military: U.S. Army

Theodore Roosevelt

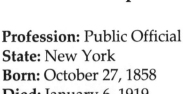

Republican

Profession: Public Official
State: New York
Born: October 27, 1858
Died: January 6, 1919
Wife: Edith Kermit Carow
Religion: Dutch Reformed
Military: U.S. Army

26th President
(1901-1909)

William Howard Taft

Republican

Profession: Lawyer
State: Ohio
Born: September 15, 1857
Died: March 8, 1930
Wife: Helen (Nellie) Herron
Religion: Unitarian
Military: None

27th President
(1909-1913)

Woodrow Wilson   Democrat

28th President
(1913-1921)

Profession: Lawyer/Professor
State: New Jersey
Born: December 28, 1856
Died: Febuary 3, 1924
Wife: Ellen L. Axson
    (died 1914)
    Edith Bolling Galt
    (married 1915)
Religion: Presbyterian
Military: None

Warren Gamaliel Harding   Republican

29th President
(1921-1923)

Profession: Publisher/
    Newspaper Editor
State: Ohio
Born: November 2, 1865
Died: August 2, 1923
Wife: Florence DeWolfe
Religion: Baptist
Military: None

Calvin Coolidge   Republican

Profession: Lawyer
State: Massachusetts
Born: July 4, 1872
Died: January 5, 1933
Wife: Grace A. Goodhue
Religion: Congregationalist
Military: None

**30th President
(1923-1929)**

Herbert Clark Hoover   Republican

Profession: Engineer
State: California
Born: August 10, 1874
Died: October 20, 1964
Wife: Lou Henry
Religion: Quaker
Military: None

**31st President
(1929-1933)**

Franklin Delano Roosevelt   **Democrat**

Profession: Lawyer
State: New York
Born: January 30, 1882
Died: April 12, 1945
Wife: Anna Eleanor
    Roosevelt
Religion: Episcopalian
Military: None

**32nd President
(1933-1945)**

Harry S Truman   **Democrat**

Profession: Public Official
State: Missouri
Born: May 8, 1884
Died: December 26, 1972
Wife: Bess Wallace
Religion: Baptist
Military: U.S. Army

**33rd President
(1945-1953)**

Dwight David Eisenhower   Republican

Profession: Soldier
State: New York
Born: October 14th, 1890
Died: March 28, 1969
Wife: Mamie Geneva Doud
Religion: Presbyterian
Military: U.S. Army

34th President
(1953-1961)

John Fitzgerald Kennedy   Democrat

Profession: Government
  Official
State: Massachusetts
Born: May 29, 1917
Died: November 22, 1963
Wife: Jacqueline Lee Bouvier
Religion: Roman Catholic
Military: U.S. Navy

35th President
(1961-1963)

Lyndon Baines Johnson   Democrat

Profession: Teacher/Rancher
State: Texas
Born: August 27, 1908
Died: January 22, 1973
Wife: Claudia (Lady Bird)
    Taylor
Religion: Disciples of Christ
Military: U.S. Navy

36th President
(1963-1969)

Richard Milhous Nixon   Republican

Profession: Lawyer
State: California
Born: January 9, 1913
Wife: Patricia Ryan
Religion: Quaker
Military: U.S. Navy

37th President
(1969-1974)

Gerald Rudolph Ford   Republican

Profession: Lawyer
State: Michigan
Born: July 14, 1913
Wife: Elizabeth (Betty)
    Bloomer Warren
Religion: Episcopalian
Military: U.S. Navy

38th President
(1974-1977)

James Earl Carter, Jr.   Democrat

Profession: Farmer/
    Businessman
State: Georgia
Born: October 1, 1924
Wife: Rosalynn Smith
Religion: Baptist
Military: U.S. Navy

39th President
(1977-1981)

Ronald Wilson Reagan   Republican

Profession: Rancher/
   Businessman/Commentator
   on Public Policy
State: California
Born: February 6, 1911
Wife: Nancy Davis
Religion: Presbyterian
Military: U.S. Army Air Force

40th President
(1981-1989)

George Herbert Walker Bush   Republican

Profession: Businessman/
   Public Official
State: Texas
Born: June 12, 1924
Wife: Barbara Pierce
Religion: Episcopalian
Military: U.S. Navy

41st President
(1989-19—)